CONTOURS
OF
FAITH

CONTOURS
OF
FAITH

Changing Forms of Christian
Thought

JOHN
DILLENBERGER

ABINGDON PRESS

Nashville
New York

CONTOURS OF FAITH

Copyright © 1969 by Abingdon Press

Standard Book Number: 687-09588-3

Library of Congress Catalog Card Number: 69-18451

Scripture quotations unless otherwise noted are from the Revised
Standard Version of the Bible, copyrighted 1946 and 1952 by the
Division of Christian Education, National Council of Churches,
and are used by permission.

Grateful acknowledgment is made to Harper & Row, Publishers, for
permission to reprint excerpts from *The Old Testament and Christian
Faith*, edited by Bernhard W. Anderson, and *The New Hermeneutic*,
vol. II, edited by James M. Robinson and John B. Cobb, Jr.

SET UP, PRINTED, AND BOUND BY THE
PARTHENON PRESS, AT NASHVILLE,
TENNESSEE, UNITED STATES OF AMERICA

FOR JANE

without whom I could have written these pages, but those who know her know how different the flavor would be

FOREWORD

The substance of the following chapters comprises the Kessler Foundation lectures of Hamma School of Theology of Wittenberg University, delivered in connection with the University celebration of the 450th anniversary of the Reformation, October 20–November 1, 1967. Included also is material given at other institutions and convocations during the past five years. Approximately eight pages are repeated with the permission of Harper & Row, Publishers, from chapters in previous publications, but they are here adapted and developed in a wider context. All the material has been recast with publication in mind. While the lecture style remains, the concerns have been developed in their interrelations. Hence, the present ordering of the materials bears no direct relation to the actual lectures.

The particular stance of the materials reflects concerns which have occupied me for some time. Historical and contemporary issues intertwine, and the intent has been to be suggestive rather than to expatiate fully on all issues or to support contentions. For myself, the debate has been between past history and the contemporary scene, with only casual reference to others working in the present. That is because I have found it necessary to sort out matters in another way, however dependent I, too, am on all my contemporaries, or how much what is said here and there may be similar to them. A short, selected bibliography covering significant areas of new recent work is appended for the sake of the interested reader.

It may be helpful here to state the historical and theological judgments which inform the whole. While there are many shifts in theology as such, the thesis here is that there have been two major cultural styles in Western history which have played their role in determining theological expression. The first period runs from the early church into the sixteenth century. The second starts in the late sixteenth century and runs into our own time, though the second style did not come into prominence until the middle of the eighteenth century. The lack of a common acceptance of this thesis is due to the deceptive way in which late sixteenth- to seventeenth-century dogmatic developments appear to be the flowering and development of the previous history of the church. But the contention here is that this is a misleading similarity, that there are times in history when the repetition of the past actually produces its spiritual and theological opposites, when shifting cultural styles dictate that repetition is not really repeating the past at all. Another way of saying this is that continuity with the past sometimes demands saying the exact opposite of what has been said, while repetition of the past determines one like an ancient power of fate and thereby betrays him into thinking he is actually standing in continuity with the past.

Our time marks the beginning of a third style, the contours and shape of which are unclear. The problem for theology is that the second style has not yet been fully seen or accepted, that theological adaptations largely take the second period seriously at the precise juncture when the third age is already

8

beginning to dawn. Since this third new style is a matter of coming to birth, we cannot see the harbingers of the new world in the old. But we should be snared neither by the repristinators of the old nor by those who so confidently affirm some facet of the transitory new as if it were either vast enough or enduring enough to be adequate.

Theological programs now can be launched only in limited ways. The possibilities are restricted, but they are open for us. Traditional theology, even the idea of a systematic theology, and the life of parishes as we have known them for centuries, are alike uncertain. Both will continue to exist, and people will live and give all the resources of their being to their propagation in their present forms. Such lives will not be wasted; but there must be and will be those whose lives are spent searching other horizons, experimenting, making mistakes for the sake of the necessary new possibilities in an emerging different cultural style.

JOHN DILLENBERGER

CONTENTS

I

COMPREHENDING HISTORICAL SHIFTS

1. Orientations as Ingredients of History

Understanding past history involves the orientations one brings as well as the materials available for examination. History "as it really was" represents the slogan of a past period of historical method. It reflected the full power and overintoxication of the contribution of the historical method. Over against the former claims and counterclaims concerning the viability of inherited truth, and the citation of accepted authorities to validate and to corroborate such claims, the historical method made context and setting decisive for comprehending both what happened and what was meant. But today we know that the orientations we bring also play their role. Indeed, there are those, like the late Carl Michalson, for whom authentic questions defined the major ingredients of historicity.

The role of orientations is apparent to anyone who deals with historical phenomena. It would be interesting to study the major Reformation celebrations, at half-century and century marks, to see the role played by cultural preoccupations in the understanding of the Reformation. For example, the Enlightenment saw in Luther a religious genius, who had opened a path toward religious individuality and freedom. The great Protestant liberal historian Adolf Harnack interpreted Luther through the issues which interested him in his own work. While he still placed Luther in the context of the Middle Ages, he saw motifs of modern understanding in Luther which, in retrospect, we see as more characteristic of Harnack than of Luther. On the other hand, Ernst Troeltsch, whose historical relativism dictated no special interests in claiming any segment of history, more fully understood Luther. But he also missed facets which Harnack saw. Hence, orientations also close one's eyes. At the very moment when certain facets of an issue or setting are seen with seering power, we become entirely blind to others.

The Reformation and Protestantism look different to us because of Pope John XXIII, though he said little directly about the Reformation. Long before Vatican II, Protestant and Roman Catholic scholars had already arrived at dramatic reassessments and mutual understandings. But they were not widely known. Within less than a decade, a decisive shift in the understanding of Roman Catholicism and Protestantism has occurred for all of us. But this change is anchored as much in our reorientations as in our concrete, historical knowledge of either Catholicism or Protestantism.

It is possible and, I think, correct to say that our new understanding is more true. The situation today is decidedly broadening, for we are not overly concerned either to defend or attack the ways in which the issues were articulated by the reformers. Ours is not a time when a particular facet of theological understanding must be defended for the sake of safeguarding the whole. It is rather a time when all facets are being explored anew, when contemporary and historical understandings are not in conflict, but appear to need each other.

Orientations are inevitable. At best, they are not to be identified either with the disinterest or false objectivity that misses the nuances of religious understanding, or with the blinders which come from too partial an angle of vision related to one's own special theological agenda. It takes a discerning faith to see what transpires in the history of the church, though much can be seen without faith and though there are historians without faith more competent than many with faith. It takes detachment to keep one's special interest from dominating the scene; but without faith or passion, so much is also missed. Secular and church historians alike need detachment and involvement, and the difference between them is largely the dominance of the angles of vision from which each works. But that is also why they need and supplement each other.

Deep within the churches born of the Reformation lies an orientation to the past that takes its style from the conditioning of the Reformation itself. While the reformers understood that the source of their conception of faith was grounded in Scripture, their polemical encounters with the Roman Catholic Church centered primarily in the understanding of the history of the church, particularly the early church. While one can make a case for the special theological significance of the early church in the light of its integral relation to the early sources of faith, the singling out of this period rests on the historical context of the debates.

Theologically, there is no compelling reason for singling out the early centuries of the history of the church as more significant than other periods. The reframing of faith and thought is not as such greater in the early period, nor is there a uniform view of its life and outlook. Nevertheless, every Protestant body

15

felt called upon to justify itself in the light of the early church or in the light of what it believed to be the true New Testament community. Anglicans believed themselves to be the continuation of the gospel of the early church in an authentic tradition, largely unencumbered by the continental developments, while the radical groups of the Reformation felt that they were reconstituting the pristine life of the early church. Congregationalists and Presbyterians attempted to model themselves upon what they believed to be the New Testament community as delineated in Scripture. Thus, in the process of claiming the sanctity of the early church, many interpretations emerged. Each group interpreted other groups as having gone astray. Each group's theological position determined the assigning of a date for such a departure, usually referred to as a fall. Hence, orientations to the issues rather than alleged historical facts determined the reading of the history.

In the joining of the issues, the Catholic claim was one of representing the tradition from the earliest times, and the Protestant attack made the case that the Catholic Church had departed from its early, more Christian nature. Given this development, the contention that one period of the life and thought of the church might be as significant as another was not a viable alternative. Nevertheless, the Roman Catholic conception of development and tradition, including the possibility that tradition is a source of revelation, in principle made every age equally significant. But if this point could not be accepted by the Protestants, it could not actually be implemented by the Catholics. Protestants saw in the Roman Catholic development accretions which covered over the gospel tradition, thereby demanding a return to or a repristination of the earlier period. In the debate, Roman Catholics were forced to claim that the point in history at which they had arrived made them the legitimate heir of the earliest traditions in a process of historical continuity.

In contrast to subsequent claims about its origin and power, the fact of the papacy can be said to be a defensible historical emergent. Extensive claims concerning its historical origin in Christ himself, and the abuse of papal power in the late Middle Ages, together called the fact of papacy into question for many. But all sides to the debates argued equally dubious claims and counterclaims about historical origins, going back to Christ. Indeed, their ways of thinking continued in history long after any living or accurate memory of the historic reasons had disappeared. Until recently many churches born of the Reformation simply felt themselves to be the direct heirs of the Reformation and of the New Testament community and therein, to their way of thinking, lay their significance. Even those aspects of tradition which were accepted were assumed to stem from the earliest times.

Cut loose from the long structural history of the church, Protestants defined themselves by stressing the continuity of the gospel rather than by continuing to stress the previous churchly mode of accreditation. But the gospel needed further definition in taking on this guiding role. Even Melanchthon's definition of the gospel as the true, inherited teaching described the mode, not the substance itself. Defining themselves to themselves and to the Roman Catholics, Protestants thus inevitably stressed and elevated doctrinal aspects far beyond what some Catholics to that time had intended in their own concern with creed and dogma. Confessional and theological exploration were deadly serious matters. Indeed, the Reformation churches felt themselves to be determined fundamentally on theological grounds. Their lives were based on what they considered to be the true teaching for early times, over against a historically inherited teaching. That is one of the reasons why doctrine became so central, and why theological differences ruptured Protestantism itself, creating internal battles as well as the external conflict with Rome.

Surely it is clear that theology is itself a product of conditioning and of an orientation which one brings. Today the discipline of theology is not so sacred as it once was nor so irrelevant as it appeared in the aftermath of its reigning period. One can now talk about theology and theological matters while accepting its ambiguous role. Ambiguity can be said to be indigenous to the enterprise of theology. Theology is not seen in so clear-cut a scope or nature as it once was. Its demise at various junctures in the nineteenth and twentieth centuries was related to the fact that many could no longer accept theology in its older, elaborative, fully spelled-out, truth-statement form. But whether over-accenting theology or rejecting it, the respective groups did not escape each other. They shared the same assumptions about the nature and role of theology, while drawing opposite conclusions.

2. Orientations as Historical Shifts

To orient someone or a group is to provide the mode in which one wishes something to be understood or participated in. If what is said bears no genuine relation to the actualities at hand, it is sheer propaganda. On the other hand, there are those who assume that the materials will interpret themselves. Indeed, they do; but the price is that the unspoken assumptions, the ones which one does not know one has, determine the realities. In a genuine orientation, the suggested modes of comprehension and the things to be comprehended are commensurate to each other or in proportion with each other. They form a natural alliance. This does not mean that understanding comes easily. Rather, the orientation helps comprehension by focusing on the leitmotifs and settings.

Since orientations are as much a part of history as the materials themselves, their formation and change represent critical phenomena in historical understanding and self-understanding. The bedrock problem of orientations is the matter of assumptions. Since assumptions are the things we assume, they are hardly self-conscious. They operate within the depths of our being, influencing the ways in which we see and understand. Even when we are aware that this is the case, there is no assumption by which the assumptions can be judged. We cannot jump out of our own skins. We are trapped in history. This need not be understood negatively. It is the very essence of our historical being, though that is not its only characteristic.

The things we assume plague our very understanding of history, for they are so much a part of it. They are the submerged part of the iceberg. It is strange that such a major role should receive so little attention in historical understanding, particularly in the assessment of the history of theology. Part of the reason may be man's reluctance to accept that there is such a large arena of influence outside his direct knowledge and control. It would be too simple to say that assumptions are conditioned. That we know. What is more devastating is that they creep up on us, that they operate without our having become aware of them. Perhaps that is why there is such ambivalence throughout history about the role of conditioning and of the unexpected, of fate and of fortune, of determinism and of chance, of the predicted and of the accidental, of permanence and of change. While opposite to each other, they stand close to each other because they are polar aspects of the very substance of life and history. Surely they are more the opposite sides of the same coin than most things so designated.

Throughout its history, the philosophical tradition has been concerned to bring this iceberg of hidden assumptions to the surface, to expose it and to analyze it with another assumption, namely, that if this iceberg were adequately seen, it would be found to have a rational character reflecting the structure of reality itself. That is why the classical philosophical tradition has been repeatedly embarrassed by the persistent presence of both conditioning and random factors. Nevertheless, the glory of the philosophical tradition has been its bringing subterranean factors to the surface for critical analysis. But it is probable that its overriding assumption—that the historical process is an ordered cosmos subject to the intelligibility of such structures—kept it from seeing or accepting the recalcitrant nature of changing assumptions. The ancient conception of wisdom came nearest, in that the wise man saw deeply and did not blink at the incorrigible. But he was predominantly saddened and, having seen to the depths, posited the real world as the intelligible world in and through and beyond the appearances.

Not all philosophy took the route here described. But it was a dominant strand, and it certainly represents the direction taken by theology in its alliance with the philosophical tradition.

Assumptions create and operate through an ethos. Philosophy and theology in the West helped to develop an ethos, in which one thought and did what came naturally. To do what comes naturally in our own day is currently both affirmed and berated; but that only means that the former context in which nature, natural, and ethos were so easily identified has been lost. Nevertheless, assumptions determine an ethos, that is, the understanding which comes naturally or easily because it belongs to the springs of one's own being.

Cultural shifts involve a change in assumptions and ethos. But for understanding such change, we have no handles. Doctrinaire interpretations of history, like major thrusts in philosophy, have tried to provide such handles or hinges of understanding. They generally provide shafts of illumination under the guise of total explanation. Single cause theories at best are exercises of an "as-if" character, providing diverse angles of vision and suggesting, "looked at from this way, it would appear to be as follows."

But no single theory or combination of theories seems to provide an explanation. One is left with the fact that Hus was burned at the stake and Luther succeeded. All the analyses do not quite tell one why, though they may illumine certain aspects. All of us have heard lectures in which professors enumerated ten points designed to explain the transition from the Middle Ages to the Reformation period. The more one knows of the dynamics of the movements of history, the less such accounts become convincing. Perhaps that is one of the reasons why the lecture method is in bad repute. Seldom in such a list does Cleopatra's nose or that of de Gaulle appear. Nor does Helen's face that launched a thousand ships. Perhaps that is because historical analysis is modeled so much on the pattern of the classical philosophical tradition in which such factors were not meant to have the status of reality.

However we understand the change in orientations or cultural shifts, they do influence how we read the past. They thus change past history. The canons of credibility vary from culture to culture. And they vary deceptively as one confronts what appears to be a cultural complex similar to one's own. It is indeed a sobering thought that such historical shifts, or even drifts, are usually retrospectively known, that they are not immediately recognized but become apparent mainly when their role is already being called into question. Hence, Hegel's suggestion that the owl of Minerva takes its flight as the shadows of night are descending may well haunt us.

3. *Theology and Ethos*

Theology too is inextricably immersed in the problem of changing orientations and cultural shifts. That all genuine theological statements contain truth is not thereby denied; but the radical contingency of all theological work is affirmed. Both the statement that cultural shifts cannot be explained, and that all theology is relative to the situation, can be interpreted as matters for despair or for hope. Such approaches are psychologically difficult to accept for those who must be sure, and a source of laziness for those who must be assured of certain results. It is a source of hope for those for whom the situational aspects of truth provide multitudinous facets by which truth may be known. There is a major gap between the statement that all truth is relative and that the truth is relatively known. With insight and effort, the latter may enrich us beyond all expectations.

The inevitability of the interrelation between cultural phenomena and theology rests on two related factors. In the first place, theology has no language of its own, and secondly its affirmations impinge upon all else that man knows and does. This double problem explains why, on the one side, there have been debates as to whether or not theology is a science or *scientia,* and why, on the other, theology took the role of the queen of the sciences. That at one juncture of its history theology too easily won the battle, not only of being a science but of being the queen of the sciences, largely provided the continuing underground tow which kept theology from being as astute about its own situation as it might have been. That it had no bag or baggage of its own tempted it to dominate rather than to take on the dizzying freedom of such possibilities. By selectively and too permanently baptizing definite languages of discourse and of world views, it lost the capacity to relate itself to a variety of such "worlds," to honor the truth which each might provide, and to see that history does provide new possibilities. Philosophically, this positive possibility is expressed in the ancient idea of the plentitude of being, in which the spillover of truth provides a glorious manifoldness in nature and in history. It is also expressed in Hegel, where history builds upon itself in every increasing actualization, even for God himself. The general unacceptability of both the particular analysis of the plentitude of being and of Hegel's scheme does not invalidate the possibilities which shine through them.

Theology cannot escape the situation in which the cultural language of a period may be either inadequate or too adequate.

23

Retrospectively, we can see that the liberal Protestant rediscovery of the kingdom of God as indigenous to theology was the restoration of central aspects that had been sidetracked or lost in the life of the church. But it is also possible to see that its moral language, borrowed largely from Kant's *Critique of the Practical Reason,* was inadequate to express the depth and spirituality of man and therefore also inadequate to the gospel it was trying to restore. It is not by accident that Karl Barth entered into the "strange new world of the Bible," where in another world of discourse he discovered that the gospel dictated and demanded contours of thought which liberalism had not supplied. The salutary emancipation that existentialism brought into full consciousness through its analysis of depth temporarily obscured the limitations inherent in its own language. Authentic existence is not necessarily identical with the philosophies which give expression to the reality.

The opposite side of the inadequacy of language lies in those historic situations where the categories and philosophical conceptions say more than one intends to say. Greek categories were so rich and diverse in possibilities, even though deficient at critical points, that the gospel could not sufficiently command them or transform them but was itself frequently deformed by them. If one were given a choice—and it is doubtful that this could be—one would undoubtedly choose the richer rather than the narrower categories. Perhaps Milton did this in his own time when he chose the scriptural world over against other alternatives as the model for his epic.

Such problems are inherent in the situation at best. The problems are aggravated when unreflective ways of thinking become the bearers of cultural and theological understanding, for then the critical capacities for assessment and change are inoperative. They are compounded when the ways of thinking in which the gospel has been given theological expression are no longer viable in the culture in which one lives. In such contexts the defensiveness associated with orthodoxy is understandably born. Orthodoxies are frequently followed by a reaction built on the urges for modernization. In both instances, world views and ways of thinking, instead of becoming new possibilities, actually stand between the gospel and ourselves.

While having no language or world of its own, religion impinges upon all of reality. That is why those who do not like the nature of a particular impingement always wish to give religion a world of its own and preface every such statement by the declaration "religion should stay out of. . . ." The nature of such impingement may be right or wrong, destructive or creative. But it is always present and never without attendant problems. It is important that theologians should not overstep legitimate boundaries. But issues always arise because the demarcation of boundaries is not clear-cut, except abstractly, and because the particular concerns of one area may conflict with another, temporarily or permanently, rightly or wrongly.

Problems are not susceptible to abstract answers; they are more susceptible to creative resolution through a clear seeing of their context. Contexts are always historical, and thus they demand a discerning eye. That is not easy, even for the historian, because he, too, belongs to the context. But it is his task, as best he can, to deal with the variety of contexts that make up history, and in this sense to be as free as he can, so that we do not simply become the victims of conditioning. The task is complicated by the fact that the historian is a participant in the very thing he is studying and, as a participant, changes the history he is studying. There is a possible analogy to this problem in physics, where some maintain that the observer disturbs the experiment, and that as a result certain kinds of information cannot be accurately obtained.

In the relation of theology and ethos it is not a matter of which is most dominant or that both are involved, but rather of attempting to discern what is taking place. Discernment is a transcendent seeing as the concomitant of involvement. As such, neither the involved nor the uninvolved see. Discernment can be said to be the light that goes on, the element of grace, the imagination, or the facets and impingements of life that have been most deeply accepted. This is what the ancients meant by wisdom, and what in the New Testament is known as discerning the signs and the times.

Discernment is an act of imagination. True imagination is not idleness nor slovenliness but carries its own discipline. Discernment may be said to be the particular discipline of the theologian. Disciplines are indeed diverse, appropriate to the subject matter at hand. That is why the subject matter itself has been called a discipline because ideally it has a discipline appropriate to itself. This may be described as critical logic in philosophy, as mathematics and experiment in science, as the power and mystery of words and language in poetry and in literature, as the precision of line and brush in art. Each discipline is itself a gift stretched by its disciplined exercise. That is why a discipline is what one does, a subject area defined by activity.

The diversity of gifts long ago made specialists of all of us.

In the process theology was dethroned as the queen of the sciences in its more ancient sense. To have a discipline is to accept a concrete limitation, but a limitation which can be stretched so that, by analogy, it reflects the potential humanity of us all. Indeed, such diversity may be essential for humanity itself, expressing the plentitude of being in our culture. Specialization is not the problem it is frequently thought to be. Rather, specific views of specialization, like views of abstract reason, have deadened and limited the horizons of a specialty and thereby limited human imagination. The interrelated cultural-theological-ethos must be understood rather than condemned. Discernment and historical perspective belong together.

In our time the historian, through his canons of exactitude and discerning recreations, helps us to transcend where we are by helping us to see where we have been, and how we have come to where we are. Today, history shares with the artistic media the role formerly held by philosophy. At one time it was the grand role of philosophy to express aspects of man's spirituality through both positive and critical affirmations, covering the range of what has come to be the distinct disciplines. Today historians have taken on that task. It is interesting that philosophy has not yet taken its own history seriously as a clue to possible directions for the philosophical enterprise. On the other hand, this attitude is understandable among philosophers who believe that history reflects a dominant discipline only when men no longer have anything important to say or to create. Part of the thesis of what has been said and of what follows is, however, that history may be an especially instructive discipline when given its special role of discernment in our time.

27

4. Theology and New Assumptions

Most ages have felt themselves to be new. Some periods have felt the new to be a distressing matter, because the new was a sign that the ancient authentic traditions were being abandoned. The residue of that historical deposit is evident in those who see each departure from accepted norms as the undermining of the foundations. But with the advent of the modern world, the new has taken on a positive tone, so that at least in principle one welcomes a new age. The question of whether or not there is anything new under the sun is hardly worth the debate, for so much hinges on the meaning of newness or originality. In the minimum sense, each age is new if one stresses the authentic nuances which are inherent in its own articulation of older affirmations or of modifications of such affirmations.

One historical point is clear. Few would deny that the dynamics created by the burgeoning of knowledge and technology since the nineteenth century have transformed our world more than the world was changed in nineteen centuries of Christian history, or indeed than perhaps the view of the world was transformed at the time of the advent of Christianity itself. That our immediate predecessors were intoxicated by this new development and turned it to advantage in a theory of progress, now so devastatingly smashed, should not blind us to the transformation that has been wrought.

It is uncomfortable but nevertheless true that we are having to accept fluidity as the lot of our existence. Conceptions of stability and order in their older sense are no longer viable. It does not follow that the disappearance of these conceptions in their older form means that order and structure have disappeared;

it means rather that different conceptions of order and structure are emerging. It may be difficult in the interim to distinguish the genuine disintegration of order from the emerging new forms. That is again a problem demanding a discerning eye. So clear is this change that a new type of humanity may be said to be emerging, one which will be threatened by the absence of change rather than by its presence.

Theology has a double problem in the modern world. It has the age-old problem attendant to being the kind of discipline that it is. But that problem is intensified in the light of the radical transformation of categories of understanding which have emerged in the modern world. It has already been said that neither the gospel, the Christian faith, nor theology has independent categories—a language of its own. Indeed, all language is borrowed. One does not need to deny but rather can affirm that the gospel itself made its advent in the shaping of the word of God; and that critical junctures in history have formed and transformed language and given it new shape and power, and therefore also new substance. But it is important that the full ramifications of this fact be understood and accepted. The gospel itself gave new substance to a borrowed language, a language which bears all the traces of its time and place. How then could it be otherwise in theology!

The problem would be relatively simple if it were merely that the older categories, adequate for nineteen centuries of Christian history, had been transplanted by new, accepted categories. The latter may have been the hope in the new nineteenth-century mentality. But, in point of fact, our situation is one of the complete fluidity of concepts, the intense increase of knowledge in all domains, and the burgeoning of new fields of endeavor. Taken together, this means that it is no longer possible to articulate a theological position which, by accumulative elaboration, would be comprehensive in the old sense, or essentially valid for an indefinite period. The dynamics of life and history are such that what can be mastered today must take dramatically new form tomorrow. This is a startling fact with which we must learn to live. For example, until a half-century ago, a theological student could enter the ministry with a theological position worked out with the help of his teachers, and find that its basic shape was valid for his entire ministry. This possibility has disappeared, and it has become impossible to refurbish older conceptions. Most of the inherited theological systems were couched and formed in a world in which ways of thinking were relatively constant.

But in spite of the surface phenomenon, we live neither in a gradualist nor a cataclysmic period, but in one in which new-felt orientations clamor to be heard and to mark out the future. That is why ours is a troubled time, indeed more troubled than a gradualist or cataclysmic period would imply. A period of gradual development builds the unknown directly upon what it knows from the past. Cataclysmic change defines itself over against something specific, and therefore reflects the spirit of what it opposes. Both approaches are intelligible even when they are in deadly combat. But when new stirrings arise in a body politic which are not identifiable by the "either-or" possibilities, or do not fit the phases of thinking and doing at hand, a new period is dawning.

There are always protests; but while they remain intelligible and produce change, they are not reorientations of culture. There are always new ideas; but while they remain easily acceptable, they do not form new periods of history. The dynamics of protest and of ideas that can neither be suppressed nor domesticated form new times—glorious, frightening, or demonic. Precisely because the future cannot be anticipated, such birth pangs tempt us to support, to reject, or simply to wait. But there is no strategy for such a time. There is only the discerning of the times, and readiness and openness to the agony of birth. There is no turning back and no sure place to go. It is a winnowing time when the fainthearted lose courage and men of faith have nothing left but faith itself.

It will be said that the Judeo-Christian heritage—a term which is itself being challenged—has always understood history like that. But it is still a shock when the very culture which such a tradition has created becomes subject to the eschatological dimensions of a Judaism and Christianity now struggling to free themselves from their own creations. This leads to uncertainty about the culture which surrounds it. While the Judeo-Christian cultural tradition is in ultimate tension with all historical achievements, it is never expressed in isolation from them. It has known and affirmed historical embodiment. Therefore, the question about culture is the question about itself.

Such thoroughgoing questioning of our certainties tends to polarize people between those who want to overthrow the past for the sake of a new utopian scheme and those who want to protect the achieved creations of the past against the corrosive present. Both are wrong. Those who want only the new do not have enough perspective and transcendence over themselves, and consequently they turn out to be the most conditioned by the past and the present. Those who want to protect hard-won truth always forget how hard the winning was and how truth,

31

while it may be forever true, is always being won. In each time and place it takes on the colorations of that time. That is why it has been said that history is overcome by history. That is why the educational enterprise is potentially dangerous, directing itself, as it does, to the revolutionary roots that sprout and take over before they are really detected or susceptible to a single deathblow.

It is hard for anyone, or for a religious tradition for that matter, to come to terms with a history that bounces like that. Between being assimilated and being an alien culture, between acceptance and persecution, Judaism has never known the margins of religious success. Catholicism, through the power of its message and thought, became the religion of the empire, and then out of the ruins of the empire itself created Western civilization. Quite naturally, it has seldom understood the opposition which grew on its own soil. Protestantism, risking and fostering the eruptions of history in the light of critical aspects of the gospel, enshrined luminous parts of it as if they were the whole; and Protestantism now alternately tries to recover the impulses which give it birth or to pretend that it has always been more comprehensive than in point of fact it has been. Meanwhile, the secular world for all its marvelous achievements, is in rebellion against its parentage and centers in itself. And we, like each of the brothers in Dostoevski's *Brothers Karamazov*, have the strands of all the others within ourselves.

The preoccupation with our separate histories has blinded us to the cultural shifts which have affected the processes as a whole. That is not to say that cultural shifts determine what we think; but it is to say that our thinking is not unrelated to, and indeed must address itself to, such unstemmable drifts.

Hardly ever is the cultural shift so alien that the spirit of man cannot find its point of creative affinity. But usually the drift—that inevitable tide that informs the psyche so that it will not be arrested—appears as the unmitigated enemy. How hard it was for Medieval Catholic theology to accept Aristotle, but once accepted how hard it became to do theology without him. How devastatingly critical the reformers were of Aristotle, but how central he became to the seventeenth-century Protestant dogmaticians who, indeed, hung onto him on natural matters even in the face of new evidence.

There are tides which cannot be stemmed, but truth is not thereby undone. It is so hard to tell whether the tides are themselves the harbingers of some new way of knowing and seeing and doing, that is, something of the truth itself, or whether they simply stand over against allegedly winnowed truth.

Such a time of shaking also has advantages, for it is an age in which the gospel encompassed in Jesus Christ again can be made free from all that encroaches upon it. Cult and organization have had the question mark of their substances exposed. The usual disposition to religious explanation has withered enough to free us of religious idolatry. It is as if God's creation stood before us, stripped of all its religious interpretation, released from the too easy description inherent in the church, tantalizingly exposed because secularism cannot encompass the secular of God's gifts. In such a time, supports are no longer confused with foundations. The foundations cry out for the gifts of men to express anew the gift of God. The time of crisis is the time of promise, although having to live with promise without discerning the shape of things to come, can be nothing short of terrifying.

33

It is also a time when one can know the grace of God which, while it is not a place, provides us with the ground upon which to stand in all places; which, while it is not something to be possessed, is present to every time of man's life. Foundations are no longer like a rock but more like the living presence when we are safely at sea. The static images and structures fail us. In the midst of the dynamics which we cannot encompass and for which our time provides only devastating analogies, the radicality of grace grasps us in every fiber of our being as nothing stands still or abides. To live in that grace rather than to attempt to establish it as a structure of thought or a socially embodied achievement or a possession of the church, is to know of the transcendent mysteries which claim us and in that process establish new possibilities strange to the eye and to the ear.

That kind of orientation is surely reminiscent of the Reformation and of Luther in particular. Historical analogies have their problems. But analogies may be sources of illumination. Moreover, they free us from the notion that history simply repeats itself or that there is no pattern in history at all. Taking the analogies of history seriously means entering into the dynamics of past periods to discern how truth has made itself apparent in its wholeness and in its restrictiveness. We cannot simply apply the past to the present, but having entered into it, we may have the wisdom to know and to see by analogy. That accounts us, not as those who were fresh-blown into the world nor as those who have only the marks of the ages upon them, but rather as those who combine the past and present as the form of their own existence. We must then enter into that faithful immersing in the past which is the basis for not being caught within it. We must enter into the dynamics of this time, for that is where we have been asked to exercise our faithfulness. It is precisely this concurrent challenge between past, present, and future which defines a historical community.

Such an orientation through the faith delivered to the saints may provide the possibility of a different context for theological work, making it possible for us to sit loose where we have held tight, not because we have decided to abandon where we are, but because we are convinced that our conditioned present needs the illumination of the light enshrined in the ages. By definition, therefore, we do not pick a place in the past on which to stand, but we look into all past times in order to enter discerningly into our own. We must abandon the notion that there is a favorite or rightful place in history, but rather assess and enter into all times and places in order to overcome history within history.

In that process, drastic shifts do occur. But they occur elsewhere than is usually assumed. It is not that great theological statements made in a particular period have been abandoned by another time, but that the redirection of world views and cultural reorientations are sometimes so drastic that they do not allow a previous understanding to be understood as it was once known. To repeat a past formulation on the assumption that it is eternal can be so deceptive that, while thinking one has said the same as the past and been faithful to it, one has in point of fact said the opposite. So-called contradictory statements made in different cultural periods may in fact be closer to one another than the repetition of the same statements from different cultural periods. It is a part of the thesis of what follows that the problem of cultural shifts has bedeviled the whole history of theology. Orientations to problems, the directions from which one comes to them, may so change how one sees the issues that an allegedly identical answer turns out to be a radically different one. Illustrations will be given in the following chapters.

II

HISTORICAL ORIENTATIONS

1. The Mode of Theology

When the word theology is mentioned most people think of elaborated definitional statements organized in some form or system. So pervasive has this conception been that those who did not work in this mold seldom called themselves theologians. While Reinhold Niebuhr spoke against the untheological character of the American churches, even he reflected this problem in that he did not consider himself a theologian but an essayist, though an essayist who utilized theological insights. Yet, who could have been more theological? By the canons which most people use for theology, Luther would certainly not qualify as a theologian. To read Luther and then a Lutheran theologian of the seventeenth-century is to experience jolting contrasts, which no series of seventeenth-century theological citations and organization of Luther's thoughts can cover or hide.

While the church has always been engaged in a theological task, theology as we know it, and assume it to be, arrived very late on the horizon of the history of the church. Systematic theologians as we know them are most characteristically a phenomenon of the seventeenth century. One can, of course, point to Aquinas, and indeed the seventeenth-century dogmaticians were acutely aware of his work. But aside from Aquinas and a few others, it is surely clear that there was little systematic writing, if by system we mean a sustained attempt to cover the range of theological perception in a comprehensive scheme of unity. For the most part, theology until the seventeenth century consisted of particular writings created because of concrete issues and threats of distortion of accepted truths. The insights of the great Augustine are hardly given to us in a sustained work of direct discourse, but rather in discursive, repetitive, rhetorical, and embellished accounts. His writings in their original form without pruning would not be published in our kind of world, were they not the works of the great Augustine.

Most theological writing well into the seventeenth century is polemical, and the repudiation of opponents is primarily a matter of getting the best of the argument. This should be understood as the mode or way in which thought was prosecuted by all contenders. It was a matter of matching insight, of comparing text with text, indeed, of winning a point on the basis of proof text and its elaboration. It was a matter of claiming the right authorities. In short, from the standards of system as usually understood, most Christian writing can hardly be called systematic.

Even Aquinas and Calvin must be assessed carefully in this regard. Aquinas does anticipate all the objections and questions which can be put to his basic affirmations. But his organizational structure is fundamentally one of putting down and organizing all the detailed points to be made and of refuting the objections one by one. Aquinas moves from section to section, not by the logic and movement of thought so much as by simply starting at other sections. The new sections, much like points in lectures and sermons, conceal the inability to make a transition while claiming to make things clear.

A stereotype also exists about Calvin's *Institutes,* namely, that it is a great systematic work. But Calvin can be said to be the least systematic of the systematic theologians. He wished to be a biblical theologian par excellence and his *Institutes* are like a wheel without a rim, a hub full of spokes. Every theological point is hammered out along the spoke from the hub toward its end, and some spokes are longer than others. There is no rim which connects the ends of the spokes, hence no system in the sense in which we use it. The rim would be most unsymmetrical, analogically most unsystematic.

This is not a criticism, but an affirmation that Calvin, as long as the dictates of faith and scripture so demanded, was willing to leave the edges, circumference, and contours uneven. If Calvin or Augustine had actually been interested in a systematic theology as such, each would certainly have found the time to reorganize his materials more drastically than he did. Many of our problems of interpretation would not exist if the time had been taken to do the drastic redrafting that was necessary. Calvin's pilgrimage was simply that the *Institutes,* started as an aid to understanding scriptures, grew and grew until it became the interpretation of scripture. Indeed, for some it became a substitute for scripture. The final division of the material into four books, with appropriate chapters and sections, does not make it systematic. Indeed, the history of the various editions of the *Institutes* and the revisions reflect an organizational problem which Calvin never successfully solved.

If theology is understood as a system which evenly, thoroughly, and consistently covers the terrain, we must see its classical expression in the seventeenth-century Protestant development. The historical reasons for this emergence will concern us later. Descriptively analyzed, seventeenth-century continental theology, as seventeenth-century general and political philosophy, was built on the assumption that a total and complete picture of reality could be delineated. It had a grand vision of the whole, in which everything had its appropriate place. Theology then could be the queen of the sciences, ruling in every respect, putting everything in its rightful place. While we strive for a vision of the whole because we think we have lost it, seventeenth-century dogmaticians so assumed the vision of the whole that they simply started with it. Their theological method was one of making the proper distinctions and divisions and subdivisions within it.

Theological method was the exercise of putting everything in its appropriate place. "Common places" they were called. Important was the order of the problems or topics to be discussed, and once the material was properly ordered, the battle of theological substance was won. It was a crucial problem, for instance, whether the topic of predestination preceded or followed that of creation. Order or place obviously says something about content, but in this type of theology it determined its content. Indeed, where there was agreement on the topics and their ordering, there was hardly any way of distinguishing one theologian from another on the basis of what was actually said about any particular concept. The theological problem was making the right distinctions, finding the right classifications, delineating the right places. This was, of course, not a novel method, but one born out of an ancient heritage, now revived particularly through the new look at antiquity, in this instance, through

Cicero's writings. The powerful hold of this theological method is evident even in its dissolution, for it has brought us the word "commonplace." This term originally expressed a discerning art, not a commonly accepted trite truism. Two things were particularly characteristic of this form of theology. First, it was comprehensive and sought to relate itself to the whole domain of knowledge. Second, theological statements defined reality, for thought and reality were considered identical.

It has been maintained in these chapters that this type of comprehensive theology appeared late within Christian history, and that some of the great figures who are usually identified with such theologies, like Aquinas and Calvin, operate in a quite different context. Similarities seen between such figures and seventeenth-century theologies are deceptive. There are greater stylistic differences between such figures and seventeenth-century theologians, even when the content seems similar, than between seventeenth-century theologies and the eighteenth-century reactions to them. In the latter instance the divergent answers are still based on common assumptions. The direction of theology from the seventeenth century to the present will subsequently be analyzed in these terms.

It is our task now to show that, while the theologies preceding the seventeenth century were different from those which developed in the seventeenth century, a type of world was nevertheless being formed which made seventeenth-century theology at once the culmination and radical shift of its predecessors. This double aspect is evident in the fact that historians divide, or cannot decide, whether the seventeenth century is the end of an older period or the beginning of a new one (e.g., Carl Becker, Crane Brinton). The thesis suggested here is that,

41

while the seventeenth century represents the consolidation of previous affirmations, these turn out to be actually different from previous articulations, because the problems are now approached from angles of vision and orientation which reflect a hundred-and-eighty-degree shift. Hence the same formulations do not mean the same; indeed, they mean something quite different. At the same time, what is generally new is only inchoately present and does not come to clarity until the eighteenth century.

We must carefully distinguish three levels: (1) the orientation to theological issues prior to the seventeenth century; (2) the use of the same materials by the seventeenth century from another orientation; (3) the emergence during the eighteenth century of an emancipating freedom from the past only inchoately present in the seventeenth century. These levels are not identified with the three ages delineated in the Foreword. They cover only the first two ages.

2. Order as Deliverance and Threat

Order and structure are as natural to most of us as breathing. Even the new regard for dynamics and change assumes dependabilities and realms of order. While orderliness need not be understood in rigid doctrinaire terms, it purveys the feeling of reliability. The threats of disorder and the eruptive forces of nature and of history have not until recently basically challenged the inherited and assumed conception of order.

But this mind set toward the world was the product of a long achievement. For the ancients, the caprices of nature and of history were so keenly felt that they longed for dependability.

At best, permanence and order belonged to the world behind the world of appearances. The closest empirical analogue to such hoped-for order was the apparent orderliness of the cosmos. That is why the word cosmological was so significant. The Greek historian Herodotus hoped that the domain of history might have the order of the cosmos and lamented that it did not. Thucydides, reflecting upon the cycles of wars, could not reach beyond the fact of power—hardly a conception of order. The Romans, reflecting less upon history and nature than the Greeks, created an empire and an order of history without tortured concern for metaphysics and cosmological problems. Surely, success in creating relative stability and order lay behind the aura of divinity ascribed to rulers, for while they could become tyrants, they kept the world from anarchy. Empires had ultimate significance because they guaranteed an order which no one felt to be the actual order of existence. Plato's *Republic* had hovered between the ultimate and the proximate, and the haunting question of its realizability is related to the feeling that the obvious world of existence is not dependable. But it was destiny that sent Aeneas from the arms of Dido to found eternal Rome!

But Rome was not eternal. When external and internal forces led to the dissolution of the empire, it was not an ordinary crisis of history, but a crisis of meaning and of stability. It was as if the divine meaning and structure had been taken away.

The significance of Augustine lies in this setting. While giving the empire its due as a system of order, he pulled the props from underneath its divine and religious significance, brought perspective to bear upon the trials and tribulations of its history, and challenged its idealized portrait of itself.

The city of God is eternal; the city of man is terrestrial. The city of man serves man. It is a place of lesser order and lesser harmony, but harmony and order are still its meaning. Augustine was thus neither optimistic nor cynical about empire, though he is frequently read in the latter vein. Augustine can be said to have rehabilitated man in a world when man's meaning was threatened by his loss of stability. Man belonged to the city of God while he dwelled on the city of earth and labored ceaselessly in that realm.

Augustine's ambivalence about whether the city of God could be identified with the church left succeeding centuries with a host of problems. It is also clear that the political intrigue and finesse of the church, accomplished in the light of Augustine's occasional identification of church and kingdom, nevertheless created a subsequent Christian civilization which filled the vacuum created by the loss of empire. Its power in turn led to the making and breaking of political powers, and to subsequent struggles of church and state. These struggles are themselves the product of the civilization built under the aegis of the church in the light of the demise of the empire.

It is not our task here to enter into those conflicts; but beneath them one point is still clear. The development of this Christian culture fused the concerns of heaven and earth, of nature and of history, into one dependable order. In spite of a widely recognized diversity in the Middle Ages, its single thrust was the unity of all things with everything having its appropriate place. The feudal order, the order of church and empire, the order of the heavens, in spite of all the distinctions that can be made between them, were considered analogous to one another and finally reflected one order, the kingdom itself. The heavenly city of the eighteenth-century philosophers, to use the term in the title of Carl Becker's excellent book, is the residual deposit in philosophical terms of this previous set toward all in heaven and on earth. This medieval world had been taken by storm. It was a total ordering of the world in which things were made dependable, in which caprice was reduced to a minimum, in which hierarchial order was to give everything its due.

The hoped-for order had at long last come to pass. Philosophy, theology, and life were one. The view of the world and the realities at hand were commensurate with and proportionate to each other. Faith and evidence seemed to coincide. While one initially believed in order to understand, one could also now understand in order to believe, though the latter alternative was accepted only within circumscribed limits. There were, of course, still demons and devils around, and even God occasionally dipped into the order; but that was not a matter for concern. It was more significant that disorder and the chaos of nature and history had largely been purged, that the demons had been exorcised, that the world was not under the influence of powers; indeed, it was God's world, the place where his reign held sway. Such a comforting, determined order set over against the dark powers of fate and fortune is powerfully expressed in Augustine and relentlessly hammered out by John Calvin. The conception of order was a victory won, not a problem for philosophical or theological debate.

This social, political, theological conception of order was not without its philosophical base. As the Greek most concerned with nature and history, Aristotle—in spite of sporadic debates about his role—became the philosopher who still formed most thinking upon such issues well into the seventeenth century. While Aristotle represented a total philosophical view, his interest in analysis and classification, in setting forth what could be reasonably known in the range of man's life and concerns, provided the framework for linking the ultimate and the immediate. Moreover, he provided materials which could be incorporated into other viewpoints, with whatever emendation was necessary, forming the Ptolemaic-Aristotelian-Christian view of the world. However widely philosophical currents might diverge on matters of nature, Aristotle came to reign supreme. He had received Christian baptism because he provided the kind of structured order so sought by man.

Western civilization was a stupendous achievement, and its power and its hold upon the psyches of men should not be underestimated. Theological party debates, including the question of which philosophical position was most true, were stirrings in the midst of a common actual belief that order and stability were real. For a world that longed for order over against the caprices of history and of nature and the dark powers of fate and of fortune, the total organization of Western culture under the aegis of the political power of the church expressed a new structure in which God's reign and dominion were felt to be assured. In this church-dominated structure each person had a dependable place within the ordered, structured whole. Such a longed-for vision appeared to have become reality, a reality in the midst of which discordant notes were but strident aspects not yet adequately shaped or placed. Newton's seventeenth-century vision of a world essentially ordered, needing only minor mopping-up operations, was the lingering secular equivalent of this previously established theological culture.

But there is a shift in orientation between the Middle Ages, and the late sixteenth century and the first decades of the seventeenth century, which is decisive for all subsequent understanding. The period of the Middle Ages had a vision of a wholeness for which it longed, which it believed in and had partly accomplished; but it did not succeed in turning its conception of unity into uniformity. Its mood had all the characteristics of a fresh-won victory in which revelation and reason, imagination and *scientia*, the order of God and the order of the world had just been unified. It took until the late sixteenth century for these fruits of victory to become so established that they became fruits to be safeguarded and defended. What had previously been such a natural and easy alliance between the natural and the supernatural, the revealed and the natural, shifted toward debates in which the same pairs were frequently pitted against each other. But even in those debates, the assumption of one, structured, ordered whole was, if anything, more dominant than it had ever been. Only now one side or the other claimed to be the dominating whole.

In the middle of this cultural shift between the Middle Ages and the late sixteenth century stand the nominalist development and the activity of the classical reformers. Both represent significant parentheses within this cultural development. While Reformation thinking conceivably could have become the barometer and shape of new cultural shifts, the fact of the matter is that the reforming activities did not come into their own at the general cultural level. Obviously history is decisively different because of the Reformation and the events it launched. But the cultural styles and shifts that particularly influenced late sixteenth- to seventeenth-century theological work are largely formed by forces other than the Reformation theologies as we know them in Luther and Calvin, to mention only the two giant figures.

The spirit of seventeenth-century theology is identical with the total spirit of the seventeenth century. It is identical in the philosophical tradition, in Catholicism, and in Protestantism. There are actual and pronounced differences in deadly combat. But they are anchored in common assumptions. The endless polemic attempts to reach finality of definition and statement against all the alternatives do not hide the common setting. Doubt and anxiety are met by a rigorous affirmation of the accepted alternative against all others. Montaigne was not in vogue, nor was Pascal; moreover, the doubt of Descartes was but a methodological procedure, anchored in an unchallenged assumption about the positive, structural power of reason to solve all problems.

The move from the Middle Ages into the seventeenth century is thus an extension of the past, but it is also a decisive shift in orientation. The fact that the Renaissance and the Reformation stand in between has obscured both the extent to which the seventeenth century is an extension of the previous elaborations of the meaning of structure and order, and the extent to which different orientations to this issue actually determine a decisive change. Indeed, the Renaissance and the Reformation were caught within the powers of a structure of order and reason which preceded and followed. The seventeenth century is finally defeated not by the powers residing in Renaissance and Reformation, nor by other opponents, but by the very extent of its success.

This is illustrated, for instance, by the metaphor "dependable as a clock." For a world whose means of reckoning time had shifted from a reading of nature to the precision of a clock, the dependability of the latter represented a form of psychic emancipation. But when the dependability of a clock was felt to represent an ineluctable order from which no one could escape, a shift in orientation had taken place. Then the dependability of a clock no longer represented a joyful dependability, but an oppressive force.

The powerful feeling for order was given a firm foundation in the wedding between mathematical and rational philosophical positions. In that amalgam, the concerns of heaven and of earth were linked in one simple, encompassing explanation, just as in theology. It represented a natural theology, out of which natural science as we know it eventually developed. But neither those who represented the natural theology position nor those who posited a revealed theology alongside natural theology knew the extent to which they represented competing theologies resting on identical orientations to the world. Inasmuch as the skirmishes and battles between theology and the natural philosophers were subsequently seen by historians merely as issues between religion and science, the extent to which these battles occurred within a common orientation has escaped us.

The actualization of one or the other competing claims created splits within the body politic and within the ecclesiastical order. This resulted in a series of what one might call "uniformity splits," geographical areas or social groupings in which *one* conception of orderliness and meaning was elaborated and tolerated. Each group believed that to it had been given the task of delineating the theological and philosophical truth for the present and for the future. So differences had to be rejected. Theologians, philosophers, ecclesiastics, and politicians vied with one another as those who had the truth and the right to dictate its acceptance. The hoped-for absolutes, sought and achieved in a preliminary way in the Middle Ages, developed in the seventeenth century into the Age of Absolutism. While the shift from absolutes to absolutism was built on common themes, the difference in orientation made it a fundamental change rather than a continuation of the same direction.

Such shifts are easier to describe than to explain. At best, one can only provide hints. Obviously, people needed to feel more secure. Perhaps that is because disturbing historic events challenged political stability precisely when it was felt that stability had at long last been attained. We know that the fear of anarchy was greater than the fear of tyranny. The recorded psychic terror caused by the appearance of a comet or the Lisbon earthquake reflects the shock which a challenge to the newly won order brought with it. It was not so much that order was disturbed as that dark mysterious powers seemed to be disturbing it. It had been an accepted axiom that the order of the world was susceptible to suspension and invasion by its creator. God's power was once understood as working its way in the midst of competing powers. But by now it was believed that the world had been freed of such demonic powers. In the newly won order only the Lord of order invaded or suspended order. Allegedly, no other forces existed.

But as the intoxication with the mathematical order of the world intensified, even God's interference with order, once so easily assumed, became hard to accept. The confidence that the world was a rational, mathematically ordered whole gave a new dominance to the role of reason and nature as the arbiter, if not the source, of all truth. Surely Galileo's declaration that the

Book of Nature more clearly disclosed God than the Book of Scripture was a sign of this confidence. That this statement was not challenged while his astronomical theories were, reflects the hold of this view of reason and nature in the church.

In this new shift forming the rationalism of the seventeenth century, reason is associated with the new mathematics and the new science in a theory that encompasses all the concerns of man. Rationalism thus includes or becomes a substitute for theology. Philosophy, once the handmaiden of theology, now frequently made theology the adjunct of philosophy. Many philosophers said that the Christian claim accorded with reason. It was even said that the revelational incursions into the world of nature were themselves reasonable. The notion persisted for a long time that the messianic expectations and their fulfillment in Christ, and the uses of prophecy and miracle as further proofs of the Messiah, were reasonable expectations. It was such views which the philosopher David Hume unsuccessfully but devastatingly attacked, while John Locke exhibited the traditional ideas about the Messiah in an unreconstructed, secular, rational vein which he assumed to be Christian.

The ancient, longed-for order of the world, having won ascendancy in the Middle Ages as an emancipating power, in the seventeenth century took on the form of a new oppressive power with which man had to come to terms.

3. Theology in an Ordered World

Theology as we have received it is the deposit of order and structure in a seventeenth-century form. That is why it can be said that the sixteenth-century Reformation did not come into its own. The theology of a Luther and a Calvin is quite different from the theologizing in the seventeenth-century Lutheran and the Reformed traditions. The powerful hold of the seventeenth-century form of theology still operates in many branches of Lutheranism and in conservative pockets of the Reformed tradition. These orthodox theologies are hardly read. They seem to exercise their power by a form of sociological transmission. Unfortunately, the abandonment of the seventeenth-century orthodox theologies does not eliminate their influence. Only the full exposure of what they are provides the kind of historical exorcism necessary for the creation of fresh possibilities.

The mainstreams of eighteenth- and nineteenth-century theology chiefly reflect a development over against the seventeenth-century systems. Consequently, these theologies do not escape the problems posed by the seventeenth century. There is no new start, there are only new accents in an older setting. The evangelical movements of the eighteenth century tried to recapture the place of vibrant faith over against the overly intellectualized conceptions of traditional theology. Pietism brought new life into Lutheranism without abandoning its theological system. It softened the hard edges. The religious awakenings, including the period called the Great Awakening, were carried out in the context of a Puritan theology that had the contours of the older orthodoxy. The evangelical Methodist movement initially brought life in and over against an Anglican heritage whose prayer-book life was not vital but rote. However, the Anglican loss of vitality was not so much a result of a rote use of established liturgy as the product of a rationalist and at times near Deist theology. The idea that liturgy is a lifeless refrain that inhibits the spirit is not theologically justifiable, but it persists as the residue of the reaction to an Anglicanism whose theology made its prayers suspect. The Anglican rationalization was that the life of the prayer book kept direction and some spiritual vibrance in spite of a theological demise.

It is important for our consideration that the eighteenth-century thrust placed the experience of being a Christian, of the heart being moved, into the center of Christianity. Had one punctured a seventeenth-century man and asked him immediately whether thought or experience was important, he would quickly and unambiguously have answered, thought. Puncture an eighteenth-century religious man and he would immediately and spontaneously have said, experience.

The emphasis on experience worked as long as there remained a theological frame or shape in the midst of which experience found its life. But the new factor on the American scene was that, unlike Pietism in Lutheranism, or the great awakenings in Puritanism, or Methodism in Anglicanism, a wave of religious revivals swept the country at the time of the so-called period of infidelity, a time when the country experienced no theological shape. At the time of the religious revivals, experience became a kind of theology in itself. Inasmuch as these religious, evangelical movements gave the dominant form to American church life, the natural consequence was that the American churches had little interest in theology as such. But this did not mean that they escaped the seventeenth-century conditioning. When issues emerged, the discussion was dominated by the past. The result therefore was not untheological, but theological in an unsophisticated way. If it can be said that the head ran away with the heart in the seventeenth century, in the late eighteenth- and nineteenth-century America the heart

53

generally ran away with the head. But they did not thereby escape each other.

The more rational impulse in theology, so enshrined in the seventeeth century, did not disappear. A direct line runs from Orthodoxy into the Enlightenment through a series of accommodations. Essentially, these accommodations took two forms. Recognizing that Orthodoxy had overextended itself, one group gradually reduced the number of the long list of essentials to be believed. The five fundamentals—one of the sources for the word fundamentalist—reflect the orthodox rational residue. Those who could not accept this residue transformed the essentials of faith in an essentially moral direction, so that the moral, in contrast to thought and experience, became the main category of religion. While knowledge and faith had been one in the orthodox systems and in rationalism generally, Kant's great contribution neatly separated the world of knowledge (which was now the world of Newton) and the world of theology (which was now the world of the moral self).

If one thinks of style, ethos, or the shifts of culture, it is clear that none of the developments just described escaped the basic shape given to theology by the seventeenth century. Evangelicalism defined itself over against such orthodox theology. The conservative thrust narrowed the horizon of what was included in theology. The enlightenment gave it a moral and reductionist shape. While the enlightenment released new energies, it neither had nor developed an appropriate new context for theological work.

There were important developments in the nineteenth and early twentieth centuries which seriously addressed themselves to the problem of the rehabilitation of theology in the light of the world of theology created by the seventeenth century. Schleiermacher's work is exciting, precisely because it is the attempt to break into new directions while maintaining the forms of the older theology. The comprehensiveness of Schleiermacher's theological enterprise may be determined as much by his classical training as by his heritage of seventeenth-century theology. Nevertheless, he was concerned to bring each theological affirmation directly into the context of that which is known in grace. The reflective nature of theology, therefore, must always maintain this experiential context. Indeed, Schleiermacher's attempt was to put new wine into old wineskins.

But consciously and in point of fact, the heir of Schleiermacher's approach in the modern world was Paul Tillich. Here too, the old forms received new power, and this time by the combination of certain Reformation conceptions of faith combined with motifs of the classical, philosophical heritage. If the orthodox theologians felt that language grasped reality, and if Schleiermacher's theology was the elaboration of experiential grace, Tillich's theology could be said to be grace elaborated in ontological depths ranging through all the facets of man's cultural, intellectual, and historical achievements.

Surely this means that Schleiermacher and Tillich still worked within the mold of theological work given classical form in the orthodox period. In contrast, the work of Karl Barth has been closest to the intentionality of John Calvin, in which theology is the task of giving faithful expression to the nature and implications of the biblical word and world. Like Calvin's, Barth's work can be viewed either in a more traditional or in a more lively, imaginative sense. Barth, more than either Schleiermacher or Tillich, dusted off the old orthodox theologies, but he interpreted them freely. Certainly his *Church Dogmatics*, while comprehensive in intention, is sufficiently discursive and imaginative to break many of the bonds of the older conceptions of system.

Even existentialism and the existentialist theologies do not escape determination by the older theological systems. Recognizing that the older theology was built upon conceptions of nature and of structure, the existentialists were eager to bring dynamics back into theology by bracketing out the concerns of nature and by bringing the depths into man himself. One could say that the heights and depths, once affirmed in cosmological terms, are now internalized. The positive result of the existential impulse is that the horizons of theological concern have been rightly limited, though the particular limitation may be reductionist in nature. It is not a historical accident but a deliberate program whereby the current existentialist philosophers and theologians view liberal Protestant theology positively, whereas the initial thrusts of existentialism were developed in opposition to that theological position.

The existentialists can be said to be concerned with the moral in a new way. They share with Protestant liberalism the affirmation that anthropology, understood as the nature of man, is the key to theological explication. They are concerned with what is true and authentic; they share with seventeenth-century theology the passion to articulate truth and to be right.

In the attempt to come to grips with an ordered world, theologies have indeed changed at many points; but they have not found new orientations and modes. The new modes will come when theologies reflect, not that the world is disordered, but that the conceptions of order are differently conceived than had previously been imagined and that there are many other models, styles, and modes of communication than the philosophical preoccupation with the question of order.

On the current scene, theology must be approached as an orientational rather than as a definitional issue. An orientation involves contexts and meanings and is not without shape. We are at the end of a definitional period in which statements define reality. Indeed, only in a brief period in our Western history did people generally believe in such definitional possibilities, that is, roughly from the late seventeenth into the middle of the eighteenth century. In this period, it does not matter whether we are speaking about the Council of Trent, an interpretation of Luther or Reformed Dogmatics, Descartes or Spinoza. All espouse the identity of definition and reality. The residual legacy of that tradition is still evident among those today who feel that minimal essentials must be defined in a propositional way.

If we are to move ahead in theology in our time, we must concern ourselves with the totality of history, with the diverse ways in which the community of believers, the church, in fact, has apprehended the disclosure of the divine. We shall then know how the truth of a god was given to be discerned in the concrete matrices of social, cultural, historical forms. Truth is historically conditioned. It was an aberration of the seventeenth-century mind when people believed that truth could be stated finally and clearly without its historical taintage or slippage showing. The notion that God has yet more light to break forth out of his word, a positive Puritan affirmation against the overliteral identification of word and meaning, does not mean that there will be new truths of which we have not heard or that the gospel could be different than it has been apprehended.

It does mean that as a community wrestles with the reality of its foundations, the truth which has formed it also reshapes or reforms it. New aspects of truth then become manifest, though not without mistakes and aberrations. Those who want to arrest the light which breaks forth at definite historical junctures may have a passion to keep the historic faith intact; but when the older formulations are differently understood in later ages than when they were formulated, heresy may actually result in the very process of trying to prevent it.

These days, many Protestants identify truth and the Reformation less than they did. That is because they understand the Reformation better than they did. They know that its faith and insights need wider settings than a central point from which they occupied all else. Nevertheless, as we noted earlier, many churches feel it necessary to claim the authority of the early church and of the Reformation as the foundation of their lives. We must, however, abandon the notion that there is a favorite or rightful place in history, and rather assess and enter into all times and places in order to overcome truth formulations which are so conditioned they no longer have validity for us. This demands the act of discernment.

The task of maintaining the intentionality of a past theological statement cannot simply be attained by repeating the statement as formulated. It is not that great theological statements made in a particular period are willfully abandoned by another time. It is rather that the redirection of world views and cultural reorientations are sometimes so drastic that they will not permit a previous understanding to be maintained in its old form. At formative junctures Protestantism understood this, for it knew that certain facets of understanding had to be affirmed at specific junctures of history, even if the consequent risk was fracturing the historic body of the church.

Protestants who risked everything for a facet of truth have now generally lost that strong single accent and have begun to incorporate all facets of truth. This means that the same concern with faith which once accepted individual facets as the result of radical obedience, no matter what the consequences, now dictates that obedience by which the facets of truth move to their plentitude and to their interrelation. Indeed, that is the historic reason for Church Union movements. Already within Protestantism the differences have come to be more sociological than theological, though the original sociological differences were theologically exploited. Simultaneously, those bodies which claimed comprehensiveness and the tradition of the ages without decisive breaks are now open to the wider nuances of vibrant theological affirmation. Most church bodies are trying to assess the proper interrelations and thrusts of the various facets of faith. This is a new historical opportunity, where systematic and historical concerns coincide. It will demand of all of us the faithful willingness to become other than where we have been or where we are.

Many are working with a historical rather than with a philosophical style. History finds its own modes of comprehension, though they can be said to be closer to other disciplines than to the philosophical one. There is now no philosophy which holds all things together, just as there is no systematic theology which carries that function or burden. I suspect that Tillich represented the last of the great systems. The call for the integration of truth still exists, and theological schools and universities continue to justify themselves on that basis. But the idealistic, purposeful, if not willful, attempts at integration belong to an age that is past. The ideal of the Medieval university has no possibility of being resurrected, if it ever existed in its idealized form. We must accept our fracturedness together with the limitations this imposes upon us.

Fracturedness is a problem because the parts are elevated to wholes and are seldom accepted as limited parts which ask and seek for a vision of the whole but dare not claim it. Only out of limited, concentrated, daring disciplines will facets of knowledge occur which in due time will forge their own style and interrelations. These are times for working and waiting. Even philosophy has no other alternative. Once the handmaiden of theology, philosophy became the determinant of theology. But today it is as fragmented as any of the disciplines it once unified, and it is uncertain of its own future. It has itself become a series of diverse studies, tenuously confident that the dynamics of man's activities and his aspirations might become a fruitful source of exploration; and indeed they may.

There continue to be schools of philosophy whose passion for the explication and articulation of truth is as great as that of the seventeenth-century philosophers. But they have had to shrink their horizons of concern. Alongside those who hold this last-gasp position, there are those who recognize that another style of the philosophical tradition has come to an end, that philosophy too stands before new possibilities, that its form, like the form of theology, will not be a return to older systems or to anything which we would recognize as the traditional sense of system.

The social and psychological sciences, just as philosophy and theology, stand before the same problem. Among a rather large remnant of social scientists and psychologists, the passion for explanation is as vigorous as that in any theologians of the past. One suspects that much of their way of doing things is borrowed from the older philosophical orientations once associated with scholastic theology. The passion for analysis, classification, prediction, explanation describes a scholastic theology long since abandoned, and an orientation from which the natural science tradition had to extricate itself in resolute acts of severance.

The social and psychological sciences can be one of the great harbingers of common apprehension, by a humility which is interested in illumination rather than in explanation. Where illumination is sought, the horizons of one's concern are more open, both within the discipline itself and its potential relation to other evidences of human apprehension. In theological schools, those in the psychological disciplines frequently have a harder time working with one another on the basis of a difference of opinion than do the theologians. I suspect there is too much of the old-style scholastic theology left in them, and it raises again the interesting question of what is old and what is new.

III

TRANSFORMATIONS IN
HISTORICAL USAGE

Within the diverse forms of Protestantism, some aspect of the Reformation is usually considered to be of special significance for the clues which it gives to the restoration of the New Testament community or of the early church. It has previously been suggested that the particular way the Reformation and the early church are linked was forged by forms of the battles with the Roman Catholic Church. We noted, too, that this led all parties in the debate to accent orientations centered at the points of conflict. In more recent decades, historical work, freed of the polemical orientations of the past, has been able to see both the Reformation and the early church in another light. Such quiet, careful historical work on all sides is certainly the background out of which Vatican II and similar associated events became possible. Today, the early church is understood more in terms of itself and less in terms of what is claimed about it. The Reformation use and repudiation of facets of the early church has become more intelligible to us out of our understanding its inner necessity to escape innovation on the one side, and to repudiate distorting accretions on the others. But its misunderstanding of the early church, as well as that of Roman Catholicism, is also apparent.

Protestants and Catholics alike have made much of Luther's

understanding of the biblical word. Luther, whose teaching vocation involved him in the analysis and exposition of scripture, did find the crisis of his own faith solved and illumined by a discerning apprehension of scriptural passages which he understood as nothing less than the discovery of the graciousness of God himself. The contrast between this discovery and what he had known before in the church was startling. Having started with abuses, he found that his discovery had implications for the nature of the church.

But what is not always clearly recognized is that Luther found the strength and justification for standing where he did by the claim that the early church largely stood on his side. While Luther has been accused of giving a private interpretation of scripture, he himself would have been horrified by the thought; indeed, such a notion was alien to his concerns. When Luther stood at Worms, claiming both scripture and right reason, he knew that he was not standing alone. He tells us of his reading of Augustine and of others. The frequent declaration that the pope is the antichrist, a statement reflecting the intensity of Luther's opposition, rests not only upon his scriptural understanding, but upon the conviction that the tradition had been subverted to serve its very opposite. This was crystal clear to Luther by 1519, and it is expressed in the so-called Reformation treatises in 1520, particularly in *The Address to the German Nobility* and in *The Babylonian Captivity of the Church*. In this sense, one can say that Luther began a historical critical method which only later came into its own.

Debates about the nature of the early church and tradition were thus born in the Reformation itself. The discovery of the early church was Luther's final act of deliverance and provided the psychic possibility of standing on the biblical foundations he had uncovered. The gospel understanding which spoke to his own being and to his own time, had been found to be clearly present in the past history of the church. In the post-Reformation period, that is, the late sixteenth and seventeenth centuries to which we have made repeated reference, the debates also centered in what the scriptures said and in what the early church affirmed. But a change in orientation is evident. While the reformers' use of the early church was more significant than is generally realized, their use was nevertheless quite different from that employed in the subsequent post-Reformation era.

On most of the issues with which we shall deal, attention will have to be focused upon the situation of the early church, upon the reformers, and upon the sixteenth- to seventeenth-century development. The difference in mode and approach between Luther, Calvin, and even Melanchthon on the one side and their orthodox successors on the other is startling. Many of the same things are said, but the nuances and orientations are different, indeed so different that the actualities are different. The particular form of the seventeenth-century world view, which we delineated previously, certainly played its role. Exactly how that world became so dominant for theology, in the light of the previous work of the classical reformers, is hard to understand. It is one of those cultural shifts for which no listing of factors is adequate. But just as the late Middle Ages have become a new historical era for illumining the Reformation itself, so the transition from the earlier period of the Reformation to Protestant Orthodoxy is an era only now receiving historical attention.

1. Philosophy

The introduction of Aristotle into the educational curriculum of the new Protestant universities, undertaken by Melanchthon, played a major transforming role. The role of Aristotle's logic and rhetoric was soon to be followed by the use of his metaphysics. But Melanchthon is not alone responsible for this development. The role of north Italians who migrated to central and northern Europe, with their positive relation to Aristotle's works, needs further exploration. Certainly Peter Martyr, Zanchius, and Turretin demand further investigation in this regard. The use of metaphysics in the debates wtih the Roman Catholic theologians surely supplied the major context for the developments.

In spite of such factors, there is still a gulf between the scathing denunciations of Aristotle on the part of Luther, the negative judgments made by Calvin also, and, on the other hand, the extensive use of Aristotle made by the seventeenth-century dogmaticians, whose sections on natural theology were built upon him. These sections on natural theology were sometimes three or four times as long as those on revelation. Certainly, Melanchthon had something to do with this development; yet his own elaborations fell so short of the subsequent development that it is doubtful he was the villain he has frequently been made out to be.

While the factors in the development remain unclear, there is no uncertainty in what happened. Theology shared in the general cultural shift in which the structure of thinking and the structure of the world were felt to be identical. This assumption played its role in relation to every theological problem. As a consequence of that assumption, every problem was understood differently than before, even though the language, terms, and scope of the problem seemed to be the same. Believing that they had at last brought the ancient problems to classical expression, the orthodox theologians had in point of fact changed them through the tight grip of the assumptions they imposed on all issues.

By contrast, the early church had been fluid in its conceptions and in its life. The longed-for order of the ancients was also longed for by the Christians and given its own peculiar form. The problem for the early church was not how to gain one position, but how to order the diverse and multiple forms that its faith might take. The religious possibilities were legion, ranging from cultic groups to philosophical schools. That philosophy in its great classical period had come to an end by this time need not concern us. But we must note that it was followed by the development of many popular schools of philosophy, many accenting their religious character. In that setting it was natural that Clement and Origen should establish a school modeled on the philosophical popular academies, and that Justin Martyr should think of Christianity as a philosophy and consequently himself continue to wear the philosopher's gown. The sharp line between philosophy and theology did not exist, for philosophy entailed a vision of the world which included religious issues. Thus, it is apparent enough why the traditions of Plato, and later those of Aristotle, became so congenial to the wide concerns of Christianity.

Chief among viable religious alternatives were the Gnostic sects. They were religious in orientation but speculative in their articulation of faith, utilizing elements of both the philosophical and biblical heritage. Given the multiple intoxicating possibilities arrayed before men, Christians found the proper use of philosophy to be that of bringing sobriety and direction into choice. Indeed, the philosophical tradition may have provided the only appropriate style and ethos in which theology could be prosecuted or take form in this period.

The diversity of religious possibilities expressed in the Gnostic sects and in the philosophical schools met their demise in a philosophy drawn from the classical tradition. Philosophy, it was then said, was the weapon against heresy, that is, against the multiple religious possibilities that could have made Christianity into just another religion by absorbing facets of its being or elevating them into perspectives no longer appropriate to its total view. Surely, the fact that one age could maintain that philosophy is the weapon against heresy, as the early church did, and another that philosophy is the source of all heresies, as many in the modern period have done, expresses more than a difference of viewpoint; it expresses precisely the kind of shift in understanding which needs to be discerned. In its context, each statement could be legitimately affirmed.

Philosophy was not alone in playing a guardian role. Philosophy, the emergence of episcopacy, and the development of a New Testament canon represented the three ingredients most responsible for authenticating the genuine tradition and for its sober expression against other allegedly exotic possibilities. Since philosophy encompassed all the disciplines of man from art to statecraft and represented a conception of reason which included imagination and openness to the disclosure of transcendent dimensions and realities, its alliance with and use by the church were as natural as they were inevitable.

There were differences of opinion concerning the role of philosophy in the early church. But these differences should not be misunderstood. Tertullian is usually referred to as an anti-philosophical theologian. His rhetorical query, what does Jerusalem have to do with Athens, and his statements about the absurdity and impossibility respectively of cross and resurrection, themselves reflect a philosophical orientation. Tertullian stands in the tradition of rhetoric, where the impossible is accepted as true because one has not been able to turn it aside; the allegedly impossible has the canons of credibility precisely because it does not fit anything else. That which is known but is considered most impossible is therefore most true.

The statement by Tertullian, as well as by others, that we are not to seek truth any more since we have found it, is not to be misinterpreted either. It represented a position against the Gnostics, who continued to seek for endless meanings and to take every thought as a new possibility for speculation. The intention was to set a limit to speculation, for truth was at hand. The many alternative religious possibilities should now be avoided. Indeed, so diverse were the possibilities that even the philosophical tradition was more of a problem by the generous possibilities which it provided than by the limitations of its terminology. From the angle of the early church one could say that its limiting role was not limiting enough.

When one sees the issues from the standpoint of the necessity of forging a tradition rather than of maintaining a direction which is securely established, one understands why the role of philosophy in the early church is so different from what it becomes or became in the succeeding periods. The affirmations and critical tools of the philosophical tradition were used in

Christian history to forge a new culture, that of the Christian West. A Christianity confined to the cultural forms of its Judaic roots is simply not to be found.

Utilizing faith as a category of comprehension and illumination in the midst of philosophical categories provided theologians with a workable fulcrum by which the ancients and their contemporaries were "out-thought." That approach was given powerful expression in the classical formulation, "I believe in order to understand." The most powerful early use of that method was by Augustine. It received classical expression in Anselm, in which faith as a possibility of understanding is so successful that Anselm suggests that if faith were to waver, he would not be able to understand that it were not true. When Aquinas tried to build more adequate foundations for the relation of faith to the world, he did not intend to engage in more than an exercise of understanding anchored in its Augustinian roots.

It is another step—but a very decisive cultural shift—when understanding becomes a buttress. The inherited assumption that there is a God began to be philosophically buttressed—and natural theology as we have come to know it was born. The seventeenth-century dogmaticians certainly abandoned the notion that the concerns with nature in natural theology rested upon prior foundations of faith. Seventeenth-century theology, Protestant or Catholic, did not safeguard its natural theological statements in the way Aquinas did. For Aquinas, the faith orientation remains basic to all elaborations of nature. Instead, the seventeenth-century articulated structure of reason and of nature, in the midst of which reason functioned, provided a natural theology which did not need the anchor of faith. That occurrence reflected a dramatic shift both in the understanding of philosophy and in its use by the church.

Philosophically, nominalism is out of phase with this development. So are the classical reformers Luther and Calvin. While Luther naturally assumed that there is a God, he did not believe in a natural theology. He did not try to establish God's existence but assumed it, urging those who so believe to look toward his true form in Jesus Christ. Nor did Calvin stand in the tradition of natural theology. The knowledge of God the Creator is anchored in scripture, and the *sensus divinitatis,* inherent in all men, can only be elaborated at the price of idolatry.

The seventeenth-century form of an independent natural theology, shared by philosophers and theologians alike, took on a special development in the natural philosophy associated with the emerging scientific tradition. Many philosophical scientists were intoxicated by the new discoveries in nature, understanding the results to be nothing less than the delineation of the marvels of God in creation or, to use an ancient phrase, the thinking of God's thoughts after him. But the thinking of God's thoughts after him, which originally had been a matter of discerning the shapes and forms in an apparently chaotic world, was now considered to be the delineation of the very structures inherent in creation. It was the discovery of the secrets of God himself, now expatiated and made plain for man to see.

Philosophy had shifted from its use by the church as the vehicle of its faith-understanding to a totally independent form in the natural theology and rational philosophy of the seventeenth century. Philosophy now stood in its own right as a determiner of the many aspects of the theological tradition. Whereas once faith had turned philosophy against itself, even as it used it, now philosophy, with its faith in a rational structure open to the exercise of reason, determined the shape of faith. In the latter tradition, truth and statements about truth coincide, and there is no need for mystery.

2. Scripture

It has been suggested that the collecting of books to form a New Testament canon, and the developing of the episcopacy served the same function as that of philosophy, namely, the forging of the authentic tradition of the gospel concerning Jesus Christ. When the early church made reference to scripture, it of course meant the Old Testament scripture. The boundary and nature of that canon as used by the early church in different places have been debated, as Albert Sundberg has shown. The canons of both the Old and New Testament scriptures as they emerged were more fluid than the later Protestant conception of a book would indicate. Precisely that fluidity of selection indicates that one deals not with a finished product but with a process which was underway.

Reconstruction of how books were written or assembled is a tenuous matter. The more that is known, the less sure one is concerning any single theory. But it is reasonable to assume that oral traditions were written and preserved in various centers, and that gospels were written, having materials at hand. Likewise, letters and epistles were collected. Today Protestants and Roman Catholics agree that scripture is a product of the church and that the gospel which is apparent through scripture obviously formed the church. About this there is hardly any disagreement.

The second century began collecting such documents and

formed groupings which were acceptable as the deposits of faith. They were concerned with ancient, inherited traditions, for novelty was to be avoided. But if the principle of exclusion concerned that which did not belong to the authentic tradition, it still leaves unanswered how one could decide what belonged to the authentic tradition. The criteria accordingly applied were sufficiently formal to show both the success and the failure of the enterprise, though taken all in all, they reflected an acceptable procedure which worked remarkably well.

The association of documents with particular urban centers in which the pedigree of authentic missionary activity could be accredited back to the apostolic days was reasonable enough. It excluded self-styled, more recent missionary activity, in which Gnostic or other variants might have become dominant. Moreover, the association of books with writers who could claim to have some direct or indirect connection with one of the apostles provided a link which worked reasonably well. Such criteria kept out materials which might well have become part of the canon otherwise, and it also brought into the canon materials which would hardly be missed if removed. The Epistle of James, which Luther found ambiguous at the level of gospel, belongs to the latter category.

A canon of scripture can then be said to have served the purpose of authenticating a lively tradition against its overlively possibilities. The canon was not meant to freeze matters but to guide faith and its elaborations. When it was said, "it is written," the meaning was not, as it came subsequently to be interpreted, that the written was literally true, but rather that it delineated the proper continuity. Indeed, for a long time, the written material continued to be an adjunct to spoken words. The reliability and reliance on the transmission of the oral tradition was great. Writing things down was only a corollary guarantee for the adequate transmission of the correct tradition. Even as written, it served its oral purpose, for reading was out loud, even in the time of the Middle Ages. Both those who could read and those who could not found themselves oriented to understanding by hearing, rather than by reading. Even the efficacy of preaching and proclamation is related to such orientations. The role of preaching and lecturing in a reading age like our own has not been adequately assessed.

The accent in the early church was not upon what was written but on what was communicated through that which had been preserved. Allegorical interpretation of scripture was not only a matter of dealing with alleged crudities of the Old Testament, but reflected the recognition that what was written, while true at some levels, was not the point at issue, or the focus of attention. The citation of text, even the use of proof text is present; but proof texting in this period does not have the function of certifying that something is literally true but rather of connecting the present with the past, certifying that what is now being said is not novel but belongs to the old authentic tradition. Calvin still operated in this setting when he contended that the New Testament is another form or dispensation of the Old Testament. Proof texting in this period still functioned to establish connections in a nonliteral way. It was because one had discerned the connection that one could do the proof texting. When proof texting became the basis for establishing the connection, the seventeenth-century transformation of its use had brought about a radical shift in understanding.

The use of scripture as a form of discerning insight in the

73

early church was not without its fruits even on levels other than the strictly theological. Compared to much literature of antiquity, affirmations of scripture could be positively used on matters of natural phenomena, ranging from medicine to the cosmos. Scripture and philosophy shared in helping to delineate the shape of the world about one. It is not by accident, therefore, that scripture concomitantly served as a kind of book of knowledge, though the logic of its life and being rested in its role in matters of faith. There were fruitful by-products to the book of faith.

It was another radical shift when in the late sixteenth and seventeen centuries scripture became a book of knowledge, equal throughout in authority and meaning. The church's early ambiguity about the literal nature of a biblical text had meant that it never anchored its interpretation upon its alleged facticity. But it was exactly the abandonment of that ambiguity which was involved in the later claim that scripture was literally true. On the other hand, many who accepted the literal truth of scripture did not rest its authority upon that hinge. Luther assumed that scripture was true from cover to cover. At the same time he could have done without the book of James and certainly believed in a kind of canon within the canon, the gospel among the gospels. Calvin, while believing that a divine original lay behind the inherited text, nevertheless argued for the authority of scripture, not on the basis of the lesser aids of confirmation, as prophecy, miracle, etc., but upon the fact that its author is known through scripture by the conjoined connection between spirit and word. It is not unusual for a seventeenth-century dogmatician to claim that the authority of scripture rests upon the accuracy and literal statement of the text. Its concomitant and subordinate use as a book of knowledge in the early church was now superseded by its having become a literal book of knowledge at all levels.

3. *Church Order*

We have suggested that, in addition to philosophy and Scripture, the developing church order, in particular the episcopal office, formed the third ingredient in the forging of an authentic gospel tradition. The origin of forms of church order are obscure. They cannot be authoritatively delineated either on the basis of the New Testament documents or upon what we know of the early church. From what we do know, it seems that the offices of presbyters and bishops early emerged in various cities. Bishops undoubtedly came from among the presbyters, and if the bishop was first among equals, his function and status undoubtedly quickly made him first. Given the role of Rome, its place in the empire, it was natural that the primacy of the Roman See should emerge.

Theological forces too were at work. The bishop was believed to stand in the tradition of the prophets and to have particular gifts of charisma and of the spirit. Indeed, the bishops were felt to have a preeminence of spiritual gifts. When this fact is combined with their presence in centers where the accreditation of missionary activity could be traced back to the original days, their discerning gifts particularly seemed to qualify them to be the custodians of the tradition and therefore of the teachings. That bishops were considered to be the guardians of the tradition therefore was not strange or unnatural but germane to their very emergence. Hence, the authority of bishops was not one which they arrogated to themselves but rested in the very fact of their coming to be.

When the charismatic functions of bishops were not in evidence and their authority rested in the office without reference to the person, a new situation was at hand. Such charismatic gifts could hardly sustain themselves. Perhaps that is why the Puritans suggested that the full presence of the Spirit had departed from the church, that its early outpouring could no longer be expected.

The historic development at its best suggests the possibility that the symbolic office of bishop might have been the sustainer of the tradition of collegiality, not only among bishops but particularly among bishops and presbyters. Certainly this wider conception of the guardianship of the tradition was evident in the ecumenical councils and their deliberations.

It is sad when the gifts of a man do not match the office; it is a problem to all around when such a man uses the office to hide the poverty by a vigorous exploitation of the office. That the latter happens should not surprise us. We should be surprised, too, by the special gifts that grace many who hold the office. It certainly is a misreading of history to think of the episcopacy in the early church only in power and position terms. There are too many stories about priests who were reluctant to come to the major cities or who came surreptitiously, lest a hand be laid upon them to become bishop. It was certainly not the desire of every priest to be a bishop. Apparently the position was not that attractive.

There is no doubt that the misuse of the prerogatives and positions of office in the late Middle Ages colored the understanding of episcopacy. For many, the office itself could only be understood in terms of its misuse. One should recall that the reformers on the Continent by and large were not exercised or upset by the continuation of bishops in the English church, and one need only recall that the Lutheran church in Sweden has bishops to this day. The reformed tradition in England agreed on the rejection of the prelate-ridden establishment more than upon the shape which the church should take, as is evident in the differences between the Presbyterian, Congregational, and Baptist traditions.

The stereotype of the bishop as a person who claims the guardianship of the tradition in terms of the power of his office and utilizes it for pomp and show and rote activities is deep in the psyches of many Protestants. It reflects the revulsion of the Reformation period made permanent; no form of historical exorcism has yet managed to free us from it. The early Protestant alternatives themselves may have been free of pomp, but not of power. One need only recall the statement on the English scene that new presbyter is but old priest writ large.

Church unions to this day have floundered largely on conceptions of church order, particularly the conception of ministry, and especially on the attendant role, the administration of the sacraments. Other theological issues have been more susceptible to resolution. But this fact should not surprise us, for church order happens to be the place where the theological issues become incarnate in human beings and where leverage on the issues ends.

There is a major difference between the notion that episcopacy belongs to the essence of the church, understood in the early sense of bishops as the charismatic custodians of the tradition, and the notion that church order is entirely a functional enter-

77

prise. That church order is functional is of course a modern idea. Neither Calvin nor the Puritans would have accepted a functional definition by itself. They understood the New Testament conception of order as right ordering for the sake of function. Likewise the emphasis upon the apostolic succession can be understood as the accreditation of the apostolic witness in terms of the original need to keep the Christian movement from going into all directions. But tactual succession, unbroken or broken, is misplaced when tactuality is a guarantee rather than the mode of apostolic accreditation.

The primacy of the Roman See, on historical grounds, is entirely defensible. The theories which it has ascribed to itself or which others have ascribed to it have confused the more original historic realities. Whether or not it will be possible to overcome them in the decades ahead is a serious question about which Catholics themselves have strongly divided opinions.

People change ideas, even theological ideas. It is harder for them to change the conception of their status, place, and role. That is why the church is confronted by the fact that the role of clergy always becomes more theological than it ought or why, because of impatience about their role, wholly functional definitions emerge, carrying no necessary theological freight. The interrelations of function and theological ontology deserve more attention than they receive or history seems to allow.

4. Role of Tradition

In the previous sections, attention was given to the ways in which an authentic tradition was formed. Reflections upon the role of tradition are necessary in order to show that this concept also had historic transformations of meaning. For most, the transmission of tradition is associated with the continuation of the unchanging rather than with change. This is true, even though the Roman Catholic Church has been much concerned with the development of dogma. But every development and elaboration was simply understood to be the continuation of what had always been true, of what had always been the tradition. The only ambiguous issue is whether or not the development of tradition could become an independent source of authority, quite apart from the interpretation of scripture. Within Protestantism it has almost been a self-evident axiom that the tradition itself is unchanging. That was why Protestants opposed it.

The double-sided nature of the emerging tradition in the early church must be clearly seen. On the one hand, one had the forging of an authentic tradition against all the threats of new emerging traditions. In this sense, the reformers correctly spoke of the tradition of the gospel, though their interpreters certainly accented the word gospel more than its tradition. One of the roles of tradition is that its very life gives meaningful stability and direction for the future. Genuine and lively continuities define its being.

But the other side of tradition in the early church should not be forgotten either. As a lively tradition, it accented the role of change as well as continuity. Tradition emerged precisely because change was a fact. The accent fell upon the tradition of the gospel in the many times and places and forms in which it found expression. Tradition is historical. It stood against the ideal of unchanging permanence as defined by the Greek mind.

In this early sense, tradition guaranteed meaningful change in comprehending the one gospel, alike excluding overaccentuation of change or of permanence. It provided meaningful continuity against novelty and caprice on the one side, and unchanging, unhistorical conceptions on the other.

That tradition was not meant to arrest development but to direct it is evident in the modest theological guides used in the early church. The "rule of faith," so consistently recited by churchmen and theologians in the early church, succinctly covered the essentials of the drama concerning Jesus Christ. Theological writing, as everyone knows, was discursive, while the creeds were short recitals of the scope of faith. In the discursive writing of the early theologians, hardly any sustained attention is paid to the total range of doctrinal problems. On some issues, one needs to engage in a considerable culling of sources to find anything at all.

Creedal statements also provide brief recitals, succinctly covering the range of Christian affirmation. The anathemas associated with some of them exclude certain groups and in effect say those who believe such and such have no right to repeat the creed which has been affirmed, even if they wish. It was not unusual for a subsequent controversy to grow out of the over-exegetical hammering out of conceptions previously articulated, whether creedal or ecclesiastical. Hence, creed followed upon creed. On the one hand, terms quite acceptable at one juncture of the church's history became heretical at another, and on the other, heretical concepts become perfectly accepted and ᵔrthodox at another. The early church abounds with such terminological shifts. At best, such shifts created considerable misunderstanding between various groups. These shifts partly rested in the different apprehensions of reality behind the Greek and the Latin languages.

Creeds were meant to supply the perimeter of faith, not to provide statements to be believed as such. But deep within the psyche of Protestantism is an anticreedal bent. For many, creeds are to be rejected because they cannot be believed. It is granted that modern man has a problem in accepting the ancient formulations. But it does not thereby follow that the ancients looked at them in a way which is at all identical with that of a modern man, even though the ancients could have accepted them as statements to be believed. It is we who are the literalists in looking back. The problem is not overcome in writing modern creeds, as any perusal of the so-called modern creeds will disclose. Moreover, they accent the statement rather than the shape of the concerns. The ancient creeds have authority not only by the fact of their antiquity, but also by the fact of their dignity. It would help if modern creeds were written by poets and writers rather than by committees.

One of the reasons for looking at creeds as if they were statements to be believed rests in the early Reformation impulse to write confessions of faith. Confessions, unlike creeds, are longer documents which essentially spell out a theological position without giving it full flesh. They are therefore in-between documents, not short enough to be recited and not long enough to cover everything in a full and discursive fashion. While posing as confessions, they nevertheless become documents to be accepted. One is asked to confess that one believes what has been said. This, too, is part of an ancient heritage of assent to the truth of statements dealing with the faith. In fact, the early church defined faith as assent to statements of truth. There is a difference, however, between assent as the discriminating choice of a certain statement over against others, as was the

81

context of assent in the early church, and simple assent to the accuracy of the statement before one, as the later period required.

The catechisms of Luther were much more in accord with the interest in the ancient creeds. They were instructive for faith, utilizable as educational exercises. The larger confessions of faith are quite different documents. Their intention is to explicate for all time what is to be believed about the faith. Shorter creeds capable of being recited may not escape the earmarks of a historical period. But as recital, they tie one to the past. Confessional statements create problems for later periods because they exclude the possibility of encompassing and seeing their historically conditioned nature. The seventeenth-century *Book of Concord* assembled the confessional statements which Lutherans were to believe, apparently indefinitely. They are honored today much more in the breach than in the observance; but their role has never been repudiated. The vigorous debates about the Presbyterian confession of faith of 1967, strange to behold in the latter half of the twentieth century, tell us that the idea that a confession embodies truth for all time has had to give way. Indeed, that accounts for the vigor of the opposition to the new directions. In assembling the past confessions and in placing historic documents side by side with the new statement, the past confessions were respected without making their declarations valid for all subsequent believers. That procedure made both continuity and openness possible.

It is regrettable that confessions of faith, like the theologies of the seventeenth century, allegedly articulated what was to be believed for all time. That approach actually created an outlook antithetical to the spirit which produced them and to the ways in which they were initially understood.

IV

THE SHAPE OF FAITH

1. The Form of Faith

In what has been said thus far, there are two points which have particular implications for the theological task today. First, while theological work must be undertaken in what has tentatively been called the radicality of a third dawning period, it cannot be done without entering into the dynamics of the past, lest we are simply to be conditioned by the emerging present. Second, it is equally true that we can no longer repeat the past, for the repetition of the past does not guarantee the continuity of intentionality articulated in previous theological statements. In point of fact, frequently repetition means that the intention is changed, while the statements are maintained. Repetition of the same statement means different things in different periods.

As an orientation to the subsequent discussion of specific issues, it should be helpful to set forth in a preliminary form the way in which theology is here understood. This preliminary statement already discloses the way in which the actual theological issues will be articulated. In making a preliminary statement as an orientational aid, one proceeds with the full awareness that it already expresses the position which is assumed throughout, though one would like to believe that the position has grown out of the total enterprise.

Theology may be described as delineating the contours of faith. Faith is the encompassing perspective from which all that is said is seen, even though the conception of faith has grown out of the specific issues. The form of faith therefore is a phenomenological statement, that is, a descriptive one. Abstracted from but reflecting the concrete realities and issues, phenomenological description is not a least common denominator approach but a way of defining, in general terms, which is faithful to the particular realities. A phenomenological description of science delineates that science is what scientists do; the phenomenological description of theology is that it articulates what faith knows and does.

Faith as here used implies that there is a believing shape, a discerning apprehension, a lively thrust of imagination, a thinking in which things are known in, or communicated to, the depths. The deep stirrings of the human spirit are also thought stirrings. There is no independent feeling or thought, each freed of the other. Each stirs the other. The great ideas move the heart. The stirrings of the heart transform and create thought.

Faith is an encompassing concept. It is not an emotion, though emotional attitudes may be present in various degrees. The exclusion of emotion or the heightening of emotional factors are alike dangers, though even an in-between degree dare not be prescribed. Nor is faith doctrine or the things which are to be believed and accepted. We have indicated that in the ancient church the "rule of faith" was a succinct summary of the essentials, a statement which could be utilized to distinguish the authentic from the inauthentic heritage. But such a guide or rule was not a total statement of what was to be believed or how it was to be believed, but rather an expression of the scope of the concerns. Filling in the "rule of faith" doctrinally in terms of spelling out the shape, either as a result of controversy or more unpressed reflection, rightfully made things more intelligible. But the eventual identification of right statement and faith through such spelling out was a disastrous event. Faith has its thoughts but it is not identical with thought.

Nor is faith simply trust. Trusting and faithfulness, too, are its components, but they are set in wider dimensions. Trust is not a self-evident matter but represents the recognition, in various forms of both strange and familiar evidence, that one has been found of the divine. Faith is where the facets of one's being have been taken into the orbit of the divine milieu. That is why faith creates a kind of content, but at the same time takes its shape through many other avenues of knowledge. There are, indeed, many levels and ways in which man knows, and sometimes one way is more important than another. This may even vary from culture to culture. Faith is not as such another content, but it has content, both a shaping content in itself and a shape which tenuously reaches out into, and is influenced by, all that it touches. That is why the task of theology includes that critical scrutiny in which all the facets of one's being are brought into the orbit of faith.

Theology is the exercise of that particular intellectual task. But it requires critical reflection appropriate to the many levels of reality at hand. This does not mean that one is to be reflective or critical in the sense of an older logic of statement or of thought, or have a particular method applicable to all levels. The intellectual avenues are many, and therefore the critical capacities are also diverse. That is, too, why the contours of faith must be as diverse as the facets which are touched by man in all his ways of knowing.

The phrase "contours of faith" has been deliberately used. We have spoken of a shaping content. A contour is the shape of the reality it embodies or expresses. It too may hide or disclose reality, but in intention, shape and actuality are one and certainly inextricably intertwined. In contour plowing, the action delineates and is intended to preserve the reality. In viewing the world of nature, contours disclose the randomness and structured order around one. Landscape painting holds before one, as if in a moment of perpetual significance, the shapes and contours of nature. A great portrait captures the actuality of a particular life, line and shadow holding a segment of that life before one. In this sense, art is a mirror, not of nature as the seventeenth century thought, but of the forming reality in which we also see both it and something of ourselves. It is a moment or a time of truth, of being arrested then and there, of the now that illumines as life continues to be lived.

Theological work is like that. It holds faith and its dimensions before one, the mirror and shape demanded in that setting. Its contours combine so many ingredients and find the source and analogies in a range as wide as the riches of creation. The analogies drawn from landscape paintings and portraits illustrate that the facile distinctions between nature and history are invalid. In both, shape and reality may disclose or hide truth.

Now faith, of course, has to do with the knowing of God, and it demands avenues of communication appropriate to that type of knowing. Indeed, there are likenesses between the knowledge of God and other ways of knowing. But the likenesses include such a difference that in most instances they are more confusing than helpful; and yet all forms of comprehension must be included. Knowing has to do with the things of this world, and it is only through the things of this world that even God is known. It is important that such media be subsumed in order that what they disclose might be featured. Media have a tendency to intrude upon what they mediate.

A clue to the form of faith may be given in a passage from Paul, part of which is a quotation from Isaiah: " 'What no eye has seen, nor ear heard, nor the heart of man conceived, what God has prepared for those who love him,' God has revealed to us through the Spirit" (I Cor. 2:9-10). Faith is obviously beyond seeing. It is not to be had, therefore, by an examination of the world around one, even if aided and abetted by microscope or telescope. Seeing at its best is here transcended. Actually, our seeing has become very obvious, so that rather than the world giving us faith, it takes faith to see the world and its depths. But our attempt to move beyond the obvious is evident in our fascination with microscope and telescope, indeed, our current fascination with space. The attraction of the unfamiliar serves its time until it becomes familiar. But the extension of the seeing of the eye is not an aid to faith. When it was so seen, it produced the distortions of scientist and philosopher whose noble affirmations were continually confused with the wisdom of God. The eye does not see. It must be given to see.

Hearing is a problem also. In the biblical tradition, hearing may be more important than sight, and we know how until the modern world, even writing was utilized for the sake of being orally expressed. Certainly hearing is not equatable with direct understanding. Think of how difficult it is for two people

87

to hear the same thing. There is an obvious accent upon speaking and hearing in the biblical tradition, and in earlier periods of incoherent feelings and apprehensions about the things of the world, the spoken word of God brought a resonant clarity and shape to things. In an unclear age, in which we nevertheless believe everything must be assigned its place, the word of God is bedeviled by the very clarity it once brought. Now its clarity must make unclear the thousand clarities around. While once it brought to clarity, now its clarity must shake the clarities at hand.

The heart is not excluded, but it has its problems. The heart stands for the affections which inform one's being, while eye and ear are allegedly neutral. The heart is oriented by the affections on which it centers. The heart is the focus of imagination and imaginings. Heart and mind do have a certain correspondence or relation to each other. The particular passage in Isaiah speaks of what the heart of man has conceived. Many believe that the mind functions by itself, that it is the source of its own authority and provides its own norms. But in this older form of thinking, affections inform the mind. Surely the Medieval debates about the respective roles of will and intellect reflect this problem.

2. Spirit and Mystery

In theological language, spirit is descriptive of the specific nature of man and of God, and of the functioning actualities which connect them. But it is a futile debate whether nature or function is the clue to the other; they present themselves in the true sense of circularity. But precision in talking about the spirit is necessary. Is spirit describable as a separate channel communicating what one cannot secure otherwise, but a channel which has the same characteristics of other knowledge? Or if not, does the spirit represent a special kind of experience which gives authenticity because one has somehow come to know it or feel it? The problem of dealing with the spirit is that it does have to do with quite concrete content and with things which are felt. And yet that which the spirit brings to man is neither content as content nor experience as experience. It has something to do with both, but what happens transcends and transforms them. Its only analogy lies in the depths of God and of man.

It is said that "the Spirit searches everything, even the depths of God" (I Cor. 2:10). It is as if the very heart of God were defined for us by depths becoming manifest through, in spite of, but never apart from, all the manifestations of himself, whether of nature or of history, or superbly Jesus Christ. It is, as we have suggested, as if the nexus between God and man could only be spirit. It is, too, as if only the aspects of spirit connect man and man. This too Paul knew when he declared, "What person knows a man's thoughts except the spirit of the man which is in him" (I Cor. 2:11). The spirit is thus the nexus between man and man. Spirit is the aspect of man which discloses him to others in spite of what he says, which communicates in a moment, as in a glance, or in another's face, or in an action of the body. Spirit is the essence of a man which communicates itself behind and through everything else that he does and says. It is what becomes apparent through all the other apparencies. Spirit is the discerned depth.

Communication of man to man is an analogue to God's

communication with men. In both instances we enter into the depths, into what has been called deep crying unto deep. Where the depths are open, communication ensues beyond all other forms of communication.

Since spirit is not a special medium or channel, and serves communication as both actuality and medium, it is not tied to a discursive mode. But it should not automatically be connected with silence. There is altogether too much talk about communication through silence. Silence as such is not a communicating enterprise. The Quaker silence is meaningful because it issues out of a context of meanings which have been communicated. That silence through which communication occurs presupposes all the communication which man has devised. Silence consists of the spaces or the apertures through which we see because something has already been given to see through many modes of disclosure. Communication belongs to the essence of God and of man; therefore the silence in disclosure presupposes everything that has been said. It is the quiet mystery by which communication takes place because there have been avenues of direct and full communication.

The Christian faith is tied to God's groping to be known in the world from Israel to Jesus Christ. God has become known as this history has been, and continues to be, appropriated in the church. There is, therefore, a content to be received and a reception of the content. But the church always thinks too easily of the contents to be appropriated or to be received. As man speaks to man and acts in silent ways in the common recognition of mystery in all communication, so too God communicates to man in the giving of himself which is beyond all the content and all the receiving. It is this which is meant when Christians in the church declare that God is known by the spirit, though indeed the spirit is nothing less than God himself. The spirit discloses the heart of God for faith. It transforms the content which man knows and the experiences which he has, and changes both into something distinctive. The authenticating power of the spirit is present where man discerns and is given that which is true and right and good in the midst of all that is said and done. That is why in scripture one is asked to discern the signs, the times, and places.

Discernment is an art of humanity, given its power by the spirit of God. It is where men, cognizant of content and of experience, sit loose to both so they may hear, receive, and know another reality in the midst of all content and experience. The spirit is therefore not empty. God is not devoid of content or of his being experienced; but the actuality of God breaks the modes of its content and its reception. It is the mode commensurate only to God and God being known by the spirit. That is why the analogy between man and God in terms of image and spirit is correct. It is the matrix for God's communication.

We need no longer debate whether or not the image of God provides man with a capacity for knowing God. The image can be affirmed in the light of the knowing of God. Once image is understood as a capacity, it has regrettably been abstracted from the lively encounter between God and man from which we know about it in the first place. We are then in a situation in which, as Calvin puts it, man tries to build an edifice out of the ruins. But he would not know the ruins were it not for the edifice of faith itself. Hence image expresses a lively, not a possessive, reality.

Since the knowing of God is only in the depths, it is a

91

knowledge which men can check out only in the community of faith, where deep cries unto deep. The knowledge of God is not as exact as other knowledge, though it is exacting. It does not have the same contours as other experience. The knowing of God, since it is a knowledge by the Spirit, has a certitude and certainty which in some ways is more, and in other ways is less, than the other certainties of life. It is more, because it is a level at which a man risks his life. It is less, because it is illusive even while being present. God's presence is always an illusive presence, a hidden one. And his illusiveness always provides a presence which is unlike all other presence, for it cannot be taken away or given at random. The respectful reverence of God is silence in the midst of knowing. It is the opposite of braggadocio or the vulgarity of being able to declare at every point that there is a God, that there is no God; that God redeems in this way, that God redeems in another, or that God redeems at this place and at this time; and that therefore all men must be able to give times and places. God is spirit; and inasmuch as God is spirit, we must remove from men the agony and burden of trying to think of God with the categories which are appropriate to all other things, with the definitiveness of more or less. Rather where God is present, where his spirit broods, there men discern. There man's discerning is open to the problems of today and of tomorrow. There men's hearts and minds are adaptable and open because of the depths which they know.

But the substance and mode of spirit still leave us with the question of how it is that one becomes a believer. This demands an analysis which is commensurate with the concept of spirit. Many who have been nurtured in the church imperceptibly discover that they are believers, and frequently they do not know a time when this was not the case. There are others for whom having become a believer has a traumatic stamp, even datable as to time and place. Between these possibilities stand most of us, where the ebb and flow, even gradualness, is to be understood less in terms of will and growth in grace than in terms of the mystery of faith itself. But it is no less a mystery when it is a dawning recognition, or a dramatic event. Both these possibilities and others are susceptible to psychological interpretations of truth and of error.

The believer discovers himself in a situation where the declaration "then I was blind, now I see" is true of himself. To say that God's grace is readily available and man must now decide to accept it is foreign to what goes on. Regrettably, many of the Pelagian debates in history centered on aspects of this problem, giving yes and no answers where a delineation of the total actualities would have been more helpful. It is interesting that theological conservatives, who talk so much of grace, are so volitional and decisional with reference to its appropriation. This is true of both simpleminded and sophisticated revivalists.

It is more adequate to say that the gospel confronts us through its declarations, when they resonate in our world, and when such resonance finds its appropriate context and transforms us. But such positive consequences are related to the mystery of God. The appropriate response for anyone to whom grace has become actual is not to emphasize the decisions which have taken place. Rather the appropriate and instinctive response is thanksgiving and praise. It is thanksgiving that one has been claimed as a believer and in that sense redirected. The redirection rests in the work of the ground reality which has given birth to faith, to the faith which encompasses all attainments and frustrations, good and evil, and new possibilities for one's life.

The mystery of such faith does not have the characteristic of darkness but of enlightening. But where the mystery is translated into the clarity of light, the reverent respectfulness for God and for ourselves disappears. Theology and church then exist to make all things clear. Such clarity is the death of both God and of ourselves. Indeed, where all mystery has been made clear or removed, there humanity has been abdicated; and where mystery reigns, there is opaqueness but no light. Where the mystery is made manifest, the light illumines our darkness. Man seeks clarity in life and in thought, a clarity which he hopes will explain everything but never quite does. The mystery disclosed is the light that illumines, which brings to clarity, which illumines that which otherwise is dark. But it is not a natural light; it is the light that shines into our darkness. Such light finds a resonant clarity in our being. But it is not like a floodlight. It is the light that illumines even by the shadows which it casts and by the shapes and imaginations which are formed in the encounter with the mystery that discloses, the divine mystery of the springs of one's being, the divine mystery made manifest in the new creation, Jesus Christ.

Mysteries may be genuine or spurious, illuminating or obscure, permanent and clarifying of the nature of things, or open to disillusion by the clarifying discoveries in nature and in history. We have indicated that the clarifying and illuminating power of the mystery of the gospel in all avenues of man's personal and cultural expression gave credibility to the Christian claim from antiquity to the seventeenth century. Between the seventeenth century and our own time, clarity was associated with self-evidence and explanation, and its function was to disperse all mystery. Even theology became explanation, and sacramental realities became definable mysteries; and when the explanations no longer sufficed, the mysteries too disappeared.

3. Mystery and Scripture

Scripture can be said to deal with the mystery made manifest. This means first of all that the mystery has not disappeared. The claim rather is that it is not a spurious mystery, and that we know where it is and what it is like. To know the mystery is not to be freed of the veiled nature of such knowing. Nevertheless the mystery is no longer hidden; it has become more apparent.

The early church believed that there had been an increasing manifestation of the mystery from antiquity on, culminating in Christ as the mystery made manifest. Considerable stress was placed upon the clarity which the mystery brought, for it was mystery which clarified one's existence. It did not occur to them that mystery was to be eradicated. The only alternatives were genuine or spurious mysteries.

The difference in orientation between the early church and the church in the seventeenth century here again becomes apparent. In the early church, the light of the world or the truth that enlightens had a clarifying power. Instead of sheer mystery, one had the mystery which illumined. In the seventeenth-century shift, the light was not what the mystery shed; rather the light defined the scope of mystery. Mystery no longer defined one's existence but rather one defined the mystery. Now the purgation of mystery was not to get rid of its spurious and attendant aspects; mystery was itself something to be dispelled. The light and clarity which men believed in was more like the light of day or like a floodlight. What was clear was automatically accepted.

This historic development rests in the interpretation of an inherited theory concerning the clarity and obscurity of both scripture and nature. We indicated previously that in the early church, scripture, when accompanied by philosophy, concomitantly provided a more plausible theory of nature than other alternatives. Clarity of scripture served a double purpose. It made the mystery clear in the delineation of its having become manifest, and it also helped to clarify the obscurities of nature. To be sure, scripture also had remaining obscurities which were to be distinguished from genuine mystery. Genuine mystery was itself utilized as a way of clarifying the obscurity. Hence, the tradition arose that the unclear sections of scripture were to be interpreted by the more clear, a principle of interpretation which was used until well into the modern world. The assumption behind this process was that the unclear sections carry a meaning susceptible to their being clarified. It is not accepted that they may really be obscure and will have to remain such. That would not have corresponded to the dignity accorded to scripture.

The various modes for interpreting scripture are to be understood in this context. From our perspective it does not matter much whether a fourfold, a threefold, or a twofold principle of interpretation is used. Nor does it matter that several modes were used simultaneously, or that a particular problem or text caused them to move back and forth between modes, such as the allegorical or literal. The interpreters were not engaged in a sleight-of-hand enterprise, though to the uninitiated it looks that way. Rather they were engaged in an attempt to deal with the dynamics of scripture in a total way, and they were entirely right when no single mode was satisfactory.

While Luther preferred the plain or literal meaning of scripture, he variously used the traditional modes of interpretation. This is because he knew so well that a text means more than the text says. A text was to be understood theologically. He used the literal understanding of the text as a weapon against an undue allegorical extension of its meaning.

The accent on the literal text also brought attention upon the accurate transmission of texts, of having an authentic text. This concern for an accurate text was largely the product of the humanist enterprise. Luther himself utilized the new text of Erasmus, and indeed one of his cardinal points vis-à-vis Rome, namely, "be penitent" rather than "do penance," was anchored in the accuracy of the biblical text. But in itself that kind of approach was not enough for Luther. When the literal text in the seventeenth century was understood only in a literal way, attention shifted from the mystery made manifest through the text, to the meaning being what the text said in so many words.

Not enough attention has been given to the unintended negative role of the humanist movement in this development from Luther or Calvin to the orthodox period. Dedicated to the finding of ancient texts and to the accuracy of the text and what it said, it unwittingly prepared the ground for a literalistic interpretation. The transitional point may be what has been called a moral concern for the meaning of the text, as exemplified, for instance, in Erasmus. Erasmus was interested in the dogmatic and moral meanings of a text as a way of maintaining both the ancient dogma and the stability of the church while leading to its reform. In the debate between Erasmus and Luther on the problem of the will, a central corollary problem is what Erasmus called the caverns of scripture. In this debate, Luther saw sufficient clarity for faith in the very scriptural texts which for Erasmus had dark caverns. But the clarity which Luther saw in them affirmed the mystery made manifest in a way in which Erasmus did not have eyes to see. Luther's conception of clarity is quite different from the conception of clarity which Erasmus expects. Hence the same passage can be clear to Luther and unclear to Erasmus, since they proceed with different orientations. Luther, as well as Calvin, worked with what one might call a pneumatic interpretation of the text. The humanist-Erasmian direction ended with the literal meaning, in the sense that scripture was a book of knowledge to be read like all other books. Scripture could have both a dogmatic-knowledge level and a moral level. In any case, for the humanist-Erasmian reader no other orientations for interpreting scripture were required.

The latter development made scripture into a book of knowledge at all levels of content. If scripture in the early church helped to clarify nature in a subsidiary role, now its conceptions of nature gradually became as central as its conceptions of faith. In no sense was scripture to be considered as untrue. Indeed, its authority began to be defended because it was true from cover to cover. In this sense, the fundamentalists who still want the old-time religion are not old enough, because no one previously would have defended the truth of scripture on that basis, even though its literal truth was assumed.

Obviously scripture has a special role in the church. But such a role must be defined in terms other than slogans of *sola scriptura,* its role as a book of knowledge, or a source of moral insight. The New Testament canon was a way in which the gospel which initially had been carried by oral tradition was now transmitted in history. We have previously discussed the factors in the writing and collection of biblical documents. That process indicates that in principle the canon could be left open. But in point of fact, that would be too dangerous, for materials too far removed and without adequate criteria might be included. The discerning insights which come from materials that might in principle belong to scripture can, however, play their role without benefit of canon. The canonical materials provide a working norm for assessing the instructive insight of non-canonical materials without necessarily making them inferior.

Interpreting and understanding scripture demands more than meets the eye. It includes seeing the nexus between God and man in terms of the concept of spirit. For Calvin, word and spirit are conjoined; and for him this identification is the reason why scripture does become the foundation of a lively knowledge of God in Jesus Christ. One can know the content of scripture from cover to cover in terms of information without knowing what it is about. Of course, its role is also an informing one, but in a quite different sense. Protestantism always counsels one to go to scripture, as if a simple reading of scripture would be adequate. This advice is based more on the idea that scripture is a book of knowledge than it is on the reforming insights of Luther or Calvin. Krister Stendahl, commenting upon the notion that one is simply told to go to scripture, states that the Bible is the most difficult book in the world to read without help. The emphasis on scripture by both Luther and Calvin was certainly not intended as a counsel of direct access without orientation. In fact, their writing and preaching was directed to a proper orientation to the knowledge of scripture, just as the rule of faith and creeds had been used in the early church. For them scripture never stood alone. The problem was how scripture was to be understood in the church, given the assumption that it was itself a product of the church. Augustine's statement, repeated also by Calvin, that he would not believe scripture unless it were certified by the church, does not necessarily imply that church as church provides the rightful interpretation. It implies only that scripture and church are tied together, and that the interpretation of scripture rightly occurs in the church. The relation between scripture and church in this sense is circular. The interpretation provided by the church is at once the basis for an orientation to scripture; and scripture is at the same time the basis from which such orientations are changed, depending upon time and place and upon the new light that may emerge from such scrutiny and encounter. It was the reformers' contention that the latter avenue was foreclosed and that therefore they were acting in behalf of the church against a shackled church.

The orientation to preaching throughout the Reformation included comparing text with text, and frequently interpreting one text in the light of another. The reformers dealt not with single texts as such, but with the movement of texts and passages. The Reformation preachers expounded upon entire books, taking the texts in order and expounding on as many as the limits of time at any occasion allowed. Thus, while they focused on texts, they always had the total context at hand. A major change occurred when preaching later began to focus upon single texts, drawing information or religious insights out of them. In such preaching, the text became a pretext without a context. In fact, most of us have been so conditioned by the use of single texts or sections of texts that they jump out at us in reading scripture, or in hearing it read. The church might well undertake a new project designed to end that conditioned influence. Rather than to "lift up the text," one ought to launch a program for the "suppression of texts," that is, the rereading of major sections with such constancy that the text goes back into its place or context. For example, if one reads the flow of Romans 8:28 ff. long enough, predestination quits jumping out and goes back into its setting.

Scripture is appropriately understood when the role it plays is close, by analogy, to its historic emergence. Were it not for the loss of memory and for the distortions that inevitably develop in an oral tradition, the materials surrounding the events which were understood as the mystery made manifest in Christ might well have remained oral in nature. Moreover, until the advent of reading as a dominant form of information, scriptural content was communicated in ways other than the material being read silently. It is hard for us to understand that such materials were known to the common man through the stained glass windows of the cathedrals, particularly since we cannot "read" those windows today without major written and verbal pointers. The particular Protestant conception of a book could not have emerged without a printing press and the revolution this effected in creating new modes of understanding and communication.

Theologically, it does not matter whether something is oral, written, or pictorial. All represent facets of man's creativity and imagination. What does matter is that there is a shaping contour to the mystery made manifest. Without a total setting for the affirmations concerning Christ, there is no point of reference or meaning. Then as Paul expressed it, there is "only foolishness." On the other hand, all the context which man can devise, and all the patterns which he may declare to be present, mean nothing unless he has been grasped by the reality which helps him to see the pattern. When it is said that the expectations have been fulfilled, the filling of them transforms everything which was expected.

It is virtually impossible to apprehend the meaning of Christ without an acquaintance with the issues of Old Testament history. But the Old Testament also hinders the understanding of Christ as much as it helps. Hence, both those who see continuity and those who see discontinuity between the Testaments have evidence on their side. But either alternative ignores the complexities of what is involved in the "happening" in which the mystery made manifest in Christ is discerned. Where that has happened, one knows that it was not in the cards, so to speak. That is why one knows that the Spirit of God has been at work. That is why deep cries unto deep, though the depths are not a void, but a reorientation which is a having been given to see and to know. This is why Calvin's conception of scripture as spectacles, when rightly understood, is helpful. Without them, he suggests, everything looks confused and blurred. When the glasses are put on, everything falls into focus, with a sharpness and clarity it did not have before. Those who have astigmatism will know what this means. But the refocusing which occurs when deep cries unto deep is a kind of miracle. That is, it does not come about by a deliberate act, but is rather like a happening.

This is the context in which the older conception of the

inspiration of scripture needs to be understood. Inspiration has nothing to do with dictation or the words themselves, whether these be the words of men in giving the content God desires, or whether God's own words. Such an approach is the religion of the literal book. It is not by accident that some have spoken, from another angle, of a parallelism between literature, particularly poetry, and the biblical materials, maintaining that inspiration is similar to the insight which comes from literature. This is helpful; but it can also be deceptive. Those who so pursue the issue are glad that poetry, which now also is read silently rather than recited generally, takes one out of the literalness of what is said. It is true that Shakespeare grasps most of us more than does Descartes. In reading great literature, acts of discernment occur. Lights go on, and we say to ourselves, "Now I see." In this sense, superb literature is great because it is a mirror to one's self, because the author has been able to expose us to ourselves, providing the self-awareness and self-knowledge which is good because it is not ephemeral but germane to our very humanity. That is why writing which exposes limited aspects of ourselves without association with the wider dimensions of what it means to be human is borderline as literature, even if it exhibits considerable craftsmanship.

The difference between biblical literature and other literature is not at the point that one has, in each instance, been given to see, or that a discerning process has taken place. The special role of scripture is rather that, throughout the history of the church, it has become the particular vehicle whereby the lively knowledge of God has become actualized. Since this does not appear to have been lodged all along in one's own psyche, the believer confesses that more than meets the eye has transpired in a manner beyond all other literature. The things which one sees in great literature bear an analogy, for lights, too, go on. But in biblical literature the discernment has to do with the actualization of the knowing of the Divine in its broadest dimensions.

Because scripture plays this role, it may be said to occupy a special place and to participate in the ancient conception of inspiration. It is not worth a debate whether this difference between scripture and other literature involves a quantitative or qualitative distinction. Inasmuch as one knows other media through which the discerning function is analagous to scripture, one could say that the only difference is the content. On that basis, the difference would be quantitative; but insofar as what transpires essentially has no identity with anything else which one knows, it can be said to be qualitative. That debate, in itself, is not instructive. It is however instructive to know why one can pursue the question from either angle.

V

THEOLOGICAL ORIENTATIONS

1. Style and Theology

Since the time of the Reformation, a theological work was supposed to cover all the major topics. There were, of course, epoch-making works on special issues which started critical redirections that subsequently influenced the content of systematic theologies. But to have a system and to be a theologian was to cover the total range of problems.

The problem of ordering the subject matter, which was indigenous to a system, continued to exercise the system builders. Schleiermacher placed the notion of the Trinity in an appendix because it did not meet the criterion that every theological statement must, in some sense, directly reflect the experiential life of the community. Karl Barth placed it first in the *Church Dogmatics* because the trinitarian formulation expressed the very life of God and man's relation to the world. Since the Trinity encompassed all aspects of theology, it had to come first as prolegomenon, that is, the saying of everything in advance before it is later expatiated. The older seventeenth-century theologies began with sections on natural theology, followed by sections on revelation. Hence, they could follow the order of creation, fall, and redemption. For Tillich, the sections on God, Christ, and Spirit were central, but for the sake of the angle from which his readers approached the issues, he started his own system with a section on reason and revelation. He continued to make the point that one could enter into the theological system at any point since it was essentially circular. The truth in this statement is certainly that all aspects of what we know have some relation to other aspects. But as a theological method, it rests on philosophical assumptions which might be translated as a theological circle in which everything is still put in its appropriate place.

In these modern theologies, all bases must still be covered in a recognizable way. The remnant of such a felt necessity is evident among those who censor others, e.g., for not having a Christology. But that terminology no longer reflects the way in which many think about the issues formerly covered under that rubric. On the other hand, conceptions like predestination have either totally fallen out of theological systems or, when they have been adequately restated, have called into question the procedure of listing and touching all the bases. We now deal with theological issues and problems for which the older statements no longer have a direct reference but only an analogical one.

In the previous chapter, we talked about the shape and contours of faith. Faith as there defined suggests another mode for theology, in which the diverse cultural facets of man's experience may play their role. It is not an antiphilosophical position, except in the sense that it rejects an alliance between theology and philosophy which excludes all else or other approaches or disciplines. In relation to the arts, the shape of the future is not yet clear. We are at an in-between stage; we are so largely tied to verbal discourse that the new directions are still carried in the arms of the old.

Moreover, if the concerns of theology are to be more widely expressed, it does not matter whether or not what is done is called theology. If there are those for whom the *theos* and *logos* of theology mean that we dare not sever the older forms and alliances, some of us are quite willing to accept a period of nontheology. The term "contours of faith" can apply to diverse and diverging modes of apprehension and illumination.

The emphasis here is obviously similar to that of the new hermeneutic. The concern for a historical method that cuts across the disciplines as the instrument of an analysis of faith seems to be correct. But the difficulties in the new hermeneutic, as in existentialist theologies generally, from the vantage point of what is here suggested is that both operate with limited and reduced categories. These categories are fruitful when compared to those of the preceding liberal Protestantism. But they are not adequate enough for the wide range of concerns and levels of meaning now demanded. The contributions of literature, the arts, and the sciences are not sufficiently recognized among those concerned with the new hermeneutic. This does not mean that materials from those disciplines must be included. That could be mere window dressing. But it does mean that the modes of thinking, the ways of expressing the shape of things, and the feelings for the creative, random patterns in these disciplines have not sufficiently left their mark on the psychic foundations of the hermeneutical theological positions. The style of these disciplines—the arts and sciences—for expressing our humanity is different from that of the older and indeed the newer philosophical tradition. It will no longer do

107

to organize theology from the vantage point of a philosophical mode alone. This is why many artists are offended by theologians who explain a style, so that the style is no longer identical with the art but becomes deformed in the explanation. It would equally be a mistake to say, "Now we will paint," and substitute the painting for theology. It is important that the style of art or of literature, which is a way of viewing reality, be brought into the orbit of theology as style. For centuries, theology has done this with the tradition of philosophy. This was possible when philosophy included the arts and when there was no conflict of styles. Today theology must take the variety of styles into account, for by their very diversity, they reflect the far-ranging facets of the created order. That is why all disciplines belong to a theological concern. The seventeenth-century concern for unity, under the aegis of theology, reflected the validity of theology's relation to all else. But in its philosophical and rational organization of the disciplines, it suppressed the modes and styles inherent in the arts. The oppressiveness of that success is protested in the overly sensitive, strident screams of the romantics, and of Nietzsche and of Dostoevski.

At least one form of theological work could be to sketch facets and aspects of the shape of faith without being concerned about whether or not they form part of a total picture. Does a particular aspect illumine facets of our being, and in so doing, can it potentially enrich others? When a particular shape or contour is evident in one medium or universe of discourse, it may become apparent in another. The second medium may articulate the same truth in another way, and the truth may then look different for those whose ways of apprehension place them more in tune with one medium than with another. At the same time, different media may bring many facets of the same truth to awareness, facets which are not at all apparent through the other media.

Within a medium, the changing orientations and historical settings demand discerning insight. Truth always is embodied. In that sense, the mode of incarnation was nothing new. The recurring problem is that there is no way of disembodying truth in order to have it present as an essence or a kernel. There is no "in-between" stage in which truth can be seen or translated directly from one universe of discourse or medium to another. That is why the concern for truth is tied to historical analogies and to the discerning of the intentionality in theological statements. Intentionality implies sensing the truth that is being suggested in an inevitable, dynamic, slanted setting, namely history itself. That is why every abstraction from a concrete history is deadening and results in either a rationalist or moralist answer. It is also why the frank acceptance of the dynamics of history can be terrifyingly enriching.

2. The Enigma of Suffering and Disclosure

As the mystery made manifest, scripture is at once the prototype and analogue for faith and thereby also for the shape of faith. Christian thinking is therefore bound to scripture, but in the freedom of the faith which it engenders. Not all ways of reading scripture are thus identical. Some are more or less adequate; some bring forth new facets of comprehension; some may be so foreign to the subject matter that they appear as an alien body.

One way of discerning the thrust of the biblical message is

to see it as a picture of how the ground of creation, the divine, is known in a creation which at once reflects and hides its creator. The history of western theology could be written with that theme in mind, and at times it has been so understood.

Man belongs to the world of nature and of history. For the ancients, the meaning of the world included the validity of living powers and forces that impinged upon it. For our time it is rather that the world is laid bare or made secular; that is, that it is without religious interpretations. The shape of faith in scripture can be said to be one in which man's religious propensities, including the use of nature as a religious prop, are called into question. It is a situation in which God is discerned in another way, where the categories are indirect rather than direct, where they are hidden rather than directly disclosed; where there is always an "in spite of." It is as if God himself had to free us from a direct reading of creation in order to be more adequately comprehended within it. The biblical materials seem full of such analogical prototypes.

Israel's emerging monotheistic faith can be understood with reference to both nature and history and, with some justification, in that order. Apparently primitive men multiplied the powers of divinity in proportion to the powers of nature. There was a power or demigod or god for wind and rain and vegetation and fertility, as well as for those complex junctures where nature and the events of history seemed to coincide or coalesce. Moreover, primitive men undoubtedly hoped that the powers might be influenced in order to bring about a meaningful structure of existence, some structure analogous to the cosmos and to the dependability of sun and moon and stars. In that setting, the question of whether it is accidental that the God of Israel emerged from the desert was first brought to my attention by Paul Lehmann. The desert stands for the monotony of nature, where the powers and forces of nature have been reduced in number. The monotony of the desert is like the monotony of monotheism. Could it be that the sociological fact of the desert provided new possibilities of comprehension? One should not say that the desert always produced a monotheistic tendency or that pure monotheism emerged from the desert. There does not seem to be a causal relationship. However, the desert may have supplied new discerning possibilities. Moreover, it meant that the forces of nature were circumscribed, freed of direct religious interpretation. When the God Yahweh emerged, he took on the legitimate functions and powers of the diverse gods of nature. All that is being said is that, where nature is prolix rather than sparse, the polytheistic as over against the monotheistic tendencies exist.

If the forces of nature were broken in Israel's pilgrimage, so were the forces of history. Israel maintained that God had entered into covenant with a people which he had shaped and particularly related to himself. He would be their God and they would be his people. The question immediately arose, what does it mean to be his people? Surely, if they lived reasonably in terms of what the covenant implied, they should be rewarded. That is the nature of justice itself. The terms should not be too difficult, for the law made the requirements concrete and the prophets reminded those who lived by the law that it must be understood from its covenantal foundation.

For a time it appeared as though this reasonable context would prevail. The Israelite nation was gradually formed, there was a semblance of justice and order, the nation seemed to have a chance to take its place among the nations of mankind. The situation of Israel was not simply that she had enemies, as all people do, but that in relation to them, she had a special role to play because she stood related to God. Surely God could be identified minimally with comparative justice in the world, and therefore Israel's historical life could show the way of this God.

The events of history, however, were not to support this way of viewing things. A full-fledged nation had been formed, but catastrophic events ensued; the kingdom was divided, the northern kingdom fell, the southern kingdom fell, and many of the inhabitants were carried into exile. And while the political situation under the Greeks was more tolerable, they profaned the Holy of Holies, the central religious symbol of integrity. In that process, the role of Israel in the world increasingly became a problem for faith. The overly pious understood the disasters in the history of Israel to mean that the people were not obedient enough. The prophetic counsel to trust Yahweh clearly did not mean that if he were trusted everything would turn out all right, as the pious always tend to believe. Trust Yahweh, not the chariots of Egypt, was a counsel for allegiance, not a stratagem for victory. Indeed, a case could be made that the righteousness of Israel was clear enough when compared to the rest of the nations. The taunt of Israel's enemies in the midst of each defeat —"Where now is your God?"—must have wrung the heart of every Israelite. For it was reasonable to believe that God is a God of justice, a God who is good for something.

Given that historical destiny, it is no wonder that messianic expectations intensified. No good could be expected from the historical drama. Perhaps only a transcendent being who combines power and goodness could bring historical affairs to their fulfillment. The Israelites knew that the good people in the world apparently had no power, and that the powerful people were scarcely good. Only God could combine power and goodness. This seemed to be the lesson of Israel's history.

The situation was no different in individual terms. Like Israel, Job was comparatively righteous. In fact, he was attested to be blameless and upright. Like Israel, he had his troubles, and in the midst of them, he, too, was confronted by the ever-present counsel that the misfortune of one's position in the world must be due to one's sins. Like Israel in her calm moments, Job was willing to admit his own problem. The problem was the disproportion between virtue and suffering in the world. The wicked prosper; the innocent suffer. The times were out of joint. Job had only the alternatives of absolute rebellion or of affirming a righteousness which was entirely incomprehensible to him. Whatever the historical judgment on the happy ending of the story—and it probably belonged to the original story which was taken over—theologically it is not worthy of the form. If the answer to Job's question depended upon the ending, one might blasphemously reject God.

If this kind of picture is at all true, one could say that the Old Testament is the history of why it does not make sense to believe in God. A God ought to be good for something. But in both social and individual life there is only defeat, agony, and suffering. In the history of Israel and in the person of Job, comparative righteousness has no future in history.

The New Testament related that Jesus of Nazareth, for whom full righteousness was claimed, was crucified. To claim that in him Israel's history had come to its fulfillment was not easy, for in terms of the story itself one could only claim that

113

the problem had been intensified. Indeed, one could say it was a final trauma. Paul wrote in full awareness of this issue when he suggested that the Messianic expectation was a stumbling block to the Jew, for instead of partial vindication, there remained only the absurdity of total suffering.

In intention, at least, the Christians made the cross central. Perhaps God could become known as God only in relation to the enigma of suffering. Perhaps only suffering and nothing else in all creation could be free from being confused with God. Everything else in human existence came out of the positive aspects of nature or history and was in danger of becoming identified with God. If one were to look for a God, it would hardly be in the midst of suffering. A God is meant to deliver from suffering.

But the problem of the Christian movement has always been that the notion of suffering has been domesticated or distorted. A major part of the history of the church in the early and medieval periods is the attempt to explain suffering and to set it within a wider context in which everything is given its appropriate place. The radical element of the Reformation revolt consisted in again putting the cross in the center of Christian understanding and meaning. The truth that God could only succeed in making himself known in the midst of suffering had been discussed in previous periods when Christians, by turning suffering into a virtue, almost destroyed the context of the meaningful knowing of God. There was considerable courting of martyrdom in the early church. The adage that the church was built upon the blood of the martyrs is not necessarily a positive fact. For the ancients, to die well was a goal devoutly to be desired, for through such death one could erase a miserable life. It is an open question whether some of the early Christians who sought martyrdom so consciously and precipitously, were not themselves pagan in this orientation. The problem of suffering in the world is that there may be no escape from martyrdom. Augustine said, What if we were not permitted to die?

Suffering is not a good thing. To declare it good is to distort it. It may be redemptive for some people; it may drive others to the edge of existence and destruction. It may divide the faithful from the unfaithful. This is not its reason for being. Suffering is the absurdity beyond all the sin of man. It is the absurdity which cannot be comprehended and for which no explanation suffices. There is no answer to the problem of suffering.

The New Testament in contrast simply seems to say to the disciples to take up the cross and follow Jesus, the Christ. It is as if it were said that God had been there before and that the cross was the identification of one's existence. The cross certainly is a silent reminder that one may not escape the vicissitudes of existence. Even those who relatively escape the agony of the world must know that the cross is the mark of their existence as well. Between them and those who know the full agony stand only the grace of God and the accidents of history.

3. Discerning Nature and History

Within Christian circles, the drama of Israel and of Jesus Christ is considered to have implications for the entire world. When the world was considered smaller, this assumption was easier to hold. The eighteenth century's increasing knowledge of other cultures for the first time seriously and publicly raised the question of the validity of such a claim. To Christians themselves, the claim of universal significance became the background for the campaign to evangelize the world, reaching its crescendo in the early twentieth-century slogan, "The evangelization of the world in this generation." Now that we are well past the midmark of the second half of the century, that slogan and its implementation seem quite unreal.

Given the size and nature of the universe, it is apparently more plausible than not to believe in the possibility of inhabitants on other worlds. The relative silence of the theological world on this issue is salutary in the sense that the older conflicting claims have been largely abandoned. One of Augustine's arguments against life on the other side of this planet was that there would need to to be a crucifixion there as well. In a more humorous vein, a *New Yorker* cartoon of several years ago depicts an astronaut landing on a planet and, seeing a woman handing a man an apple, exclaims, "Hold off!" In imagination, the seventeenth century had developed the whole conception of a plurality of worlds. At that time it had not become a theological problem, for the known scientific evidence did not give credence to such imaginings.

The vastness of nature and the historically concrete have surfaced as issues of major import at various junctures of history. Pascal's fascination with the infinitely great and the infinitely small and man's relation to both is certainly a classic expression of this issue. What Pascal knew was that greatness or smallness was a relative issue, and that meaning and truth did not depend upon either. He knew that man was a precarious, special midpoint.

The assumption that everything is grounded in a primal reality and that that reality makes itself known in a special history or histories belongs to the Christian confession. But that statement introduces rather than solves problems. In the early church, aspects of the trinitarian problem had to do with the affirmation that the Creator and the Redeemer were one God, tying nature and history together. The concern for nature in the seventeenth century provided the possibility of a conception of God valid and uniform in his activity throughout the cosmos. Among the dogmaticians of the same period, this view was accompanied by the notion that the special history of salvation was also applicable throughout the cosmos. For the more rationalist, philosophical successors to such theologians, their orientation meant that the universality of nature and nature's God was the only real clue to theological thinking. For them, scripture could be accepted insofar as its particularities could be translated into universal dimensions of nature.

That which is discerned in the concrete and the particular is no less true because it raises questions for the universal. The concrete raises an insuperable problem only when it contradicts what is otherwise known. The idea that a particular religious comprehension in a particular form must be applicable in that form throughout the totality of the universe is the residual legacy of the domination of the older conception of nature on all issues of history. It is possible, in the midst of history as we know it, to maintain that the religious apprehensions as discerned in biblical history are more adequate and comprehensive in the illumination of our earthly situation than other alternatives, without extrapolating these for other earths or planets. The possibility of the validation of such a claim rests in the active encounter with concrete religious affirmations. There is every reason to believe that God is uniformly related to nature, and diversely related to diverse histories. A discerning eye does not demand that all issues have the universality ascribed to nature. Rather, it must incorporate possible diversities when dealing with the limits and horizons of history.

The processes of creation from the remote cells to the galaxies must remain open to scrutiny. There are indeed too many in the religious community whose horizons have not stretched. Even the question of creation as a point in time or as an oscillating, pulsating enterprise upon which no limits can be set, is itself not a theological question. But theology must be open to either alternative and indeed to others. Every last vestige of a theology which rests the meaning and significance of man in terms of a particular view of the cosmos must be abdicated. Meaning or significance, as we have indicated, does not rest on the infinitely vast or on the infinitely small, but in the apprehension of meanings which are not dependent upon either, nor necessarily removed from them. Those for whom God is a reality and for whom the Christian apprehension is true for their existence do not need to extrapolate that way of regarding things as true in the same way for the entire universe. There is certainly no compelling reason to believe or to deny that God is related to life which may exist in distant galaxies in the same way as he is to our existence. There is perhaps more reason to believe that the concreteness of historical development would make it different.

Thinking of creation in the more limited sense of our history, and taking a clue from the biblical materials as delineated in the previous section, it becomes apparent that the traditional conception of creation needs drastic revision. The traditional theological formulation speaks of creation, fall, and of the history of redemption. In order to explain the transition from a period of perfection to the realities that stand over against it, the supra-lapsarians defended the consistency of God at the price of making the fall episodic. Infralapsarians skated at the edge of God's improvisation of redemption in the light of the rent in creation. Origen spoke of a preexistent fall in order to make intelligible what was assumed to have occurred. Modern theologians, such as Tillich, described innocence and perfection as ingredients which also comprise our existence, so that goodness and distortion are posited simultaneously in the declaration that creation and fall coincide. For Calvin, the fall is a fact, but since God is responsible for everything, he can only formally distinguish between creation and fall, and God only verbally escapes responsibility for the latter.

More appropriate, it would seem to me, is to speak of the risk God took in creation—that is, in creating our type of world. Such a statement need be a problem only for those of whom risk is bad by definition. But risk may belong as much to the dynamics of our life, as the traditional conception of structure. For God to create man in his own image, to create a man who reflects him, is to create a man who could act as if he were God. The risk in creation is that man may live unto himself, that he may attempt to be as God instead of entering into or maintaining his reflected relation to his Maker. One should not shrink from the possibility that God himself did not know the outcome of such a creation. To say that God knew but did not determine the result is the wish to be omnipotent about one's own knowing; but that is hardly an adequate understanding of God. But it may be added that the risk of creation was covered in the heart of God himself. It is in this sense that we can speak meaningfully about the christological foundation of creation, the notion that all the possibilities were covered in the ground of creation itself.

If this line of approach is feasible, then it is possible to say that man, who in principle could have lived unto God instead of unto self, nevertheless found and still finds himself on the latter direction. This was God's risk. It should not be ontologically explicated or explained in terms of the dizziness of unactualized freedom, as in Tillich. Man as the image of God cannot live unto himself without disrupting his very being, for as an image he must image forth his ground and source. It is only God who is not image and, in this sense, the full actuality who could live unto himself. But God, quite unlike man, has chosen not to live unto himself, but to live in relation to a creation which mirrors him.

Once man has chosen to live unto himself, everything which he sees has lost its spontaneous, reflective character. Then the image of God becomes the haunting recollection of his source. Then a direct use of creation hides rather than discloses God. That is why God's risk in creation finds its agonizing possibility of fulfillment only where creation cannot be directly used, namely, at the common involvement in suffering. We need not be deterred in saying this because of the ancient heresy of patripassianism, the suffering of the Father. The particular way in which the issues arose in the early church was subject to heretical tendencies. But it is also apparent that the ancients so projected permanence and the unchanging into the Godhead that the suffering agony of God was unfortunately suppressed as inappropriate to God.

4. Faith and the Boundaries

The mystery of ourselves, so devastatingly affirmed in cross and suffering, poses within itself the question of origin and destiny. To the question of the mystery of creation, the Protestant orthodox theologians had a ready reply—to glorify God and to enjoy him forever. This was considered to be man's *telos,* his reason and purpose for being.

Nevertheless, the rent in creation and the process of redemption raise questions about too easy an acceptance of such meaning. Some of the ancient theologians argued that a world in which there was fall and redemption was greater than one in which the fall had not occurred. For still others, the fall, while an issue, was not really so important ontologically. Beyond nature they posited supernature or the special gifts of grace, which, while lost in the fall, were restored in and through the church.

But the question not easily solved is how far one ought to go in extrapolating discerned, present meanings into the past and future. Our very being testifies to a boundary or border mystery. We stand before an impenetrable wall; it does not mean that our existence is dark. The mystery made manifest tells us about ourselves, but it gives no reason for ourselves. The *doxa,* or praise, or glory of the One whose presence we know is sufficient unto itself or unto ourselves. It does not demand a purpose for itself, not even creation "for the sake of." The goodness of creation, in spite of its travail, is that which has come to be. The existentialist notion of having been thrown into being is a positive instinct. It need not, however, be understood in the

121

sense of a chaotic having-come-to-be or as a surd, but rather as a random, meaningful emergence, anchored in the divine. Creation can be said to be an improvisation which has not escaped its creator or the creator's mark. The eruptions of nature and history can be said to bring creation to the edge of a being thought of as a surd, to where only the christological foundation of creation suffices to give it new meaning. The ancient theologians understood these new dimensions as evident in redemption, dimensions not inherent within creation itself. But that sequential way of thinking is no longer possible. Redemption and creation are interlocked.

Just as the question of origin must remain a matter of mystery, so must the matter of destiny. In Christian understanding the concept of resurrection carries the weight of the future. Certainly the Christian faith was not born without the reorientation of meanings associated with the resurrection accounts. As Paul said, "If Christ has not been raised, . . . your faith is in vain" (I Cor. 15:14).

But it is doubtful that it is instructive for us to accept the resurrection accounts as a way of discerning the scriptural record. Paul does not record the resurrection experiences and apparently does not distinguish between his experience on the Damascus road and the traditional accounts in the Gospels. The literal interpretation of these accounts is deep in the psyche of western culture, though it would make just as much sense to be literal about the light that flashed over the Damascus road and sent Paul to the ground. Both were considered resurrection appearances, especially to Paul. It is exactly the preoccupation with the literal nature of the resurrection accounts that led to the program of demythologizing. That is why cross-resurrection has been declared to be one event. On the other hand some, like R. R. Niebuhr and Pannenberg, believe that the resurrection accounts represent a special history which functions as a clue to other history. Theirs is a sophisticated concept, a discerning of a happening which is meant to have particular significance as the norm for other events. It is wrong not because it is particular; it is a problem to many of us because the particular history is made the clue for all other history by calling it special.

The birth of faith is a cross-resurrection event in which the actuality of God becomes real, as our suffering and our life are apprehended as tied with his. For this birth of faith, what transpires in Jesus of Nazareth is analogue and prototype, the first without equal, indeed the first fruit.

To know God in this way is to be open to the future, even to be open to death. It is not that the traditional resurrection accounts are so difficult as that they are confusing and sidetracking. They place trans-worldly dimensions in this-worldly terms and therefore do demand a demythologizing effort. Life beyond death, as such, is not an issue for a meaningful debate. It can be affirmed or denied. The possibility of life after death is no more a mystery than the mystery of creation itself. But that does not thereby establish life beyond death. Those who live in faith know a new reality in their lives and they are willing to trust it for the future and for death. But their knowing ends at that point. The mystery of one's "being at all," and the mystery of what is to be, are the boundaries of our existence. The center of faith is that which we trust now, and that which we then also trust for the uncertain future without knowing that or what it will be. Certainly, to live forever could be as

123

much a symbol of hell as of heaven. Neither optimism nor pessimism about death are appropriate. Death is a boundary like the boundary of creation. One lives by the transcendent dimensions which impinge upon one's existence. They are adequate for life and for death, and for the mystery of the boundary.

VI

THEOLOGICAL ISSUES

1. Intentionality in Trinitarian and Christological Concepts

In the previous sections, considerable attention was given to the diverse roles played by the understandings of nature and history and to how these diverse modes are related in the conception of God. This broad complex of issues lay behind the older christological and trinitarian formulations. It explains why in the early church all other issues could be subsumed under those of trinity and christology. When the trinitarian and christological issues became problems in and of themselves, the broad background of their concerns was forgotten. Then trinity and christology were defended as such, for the terms no longer naturally encompassed the broad issues which had concerned man.

Today one still hears it said that trinity and christology must be protected in this corrosive age. Indeed, there are those who would determine all questions of whether one belonged to the proper Christian orbit by questions concerning trinity and christology, on the assumption that these issues are the pivotal points for faith. Others exhibit a general disinterest in the issues as such, except as they become interesting problems as charges of heresy are hurled about. Still others instinctively

125

believe that the real issues in theology are not the inherited trinitarian-christological problems. We have suggested that the early church consciously utilized these formulations in developing an entire theological position; but one could just as accurately say that the early church had no conscious interest in the problems of history or of providence as such. The total concerns of the early church could be subsumed under the trinitarian-christological problem. But when the concerns expressed in the early church are dealt with in the modern age without subsuming them under trinity and christology, one should not automatically conclude that the faith has been forsaken and that the old yardsticks must be reinstated. That would return one to a definitional, rather than an orientational, phase of work. While we must be concerned with the full scope of Christian comprehension, different ages do accent different conceptions and issues and, each in turn, will subsume certain issues under the more dominant motifs which concern them.

The acceptance or rejection of the trinitarian-christological formulations should not be regarded as a critical issue. We must be concerned with the intentionality in such formulas, that is, the apprehension of the divine presence and meaning in a particular context. Different contexts do not invalidate the intentionality of statements, but they do give the same truths a wider range of manifestation, sometimes more adequate, at other times less adequate.

While the trinitarian debates were couched in technical terms which now demand a disciplined study in order to understand them at all, in our context the trinitarian issue is basically simple. It arose as the attempt to safeguard the monotheism of God against the polytheistic actualities and possibilities in the empire. Confronted by the discrepancies between the created order and its hoped-for possibilities, some had denigrated creation and addressed themselves to the possibilities by which men might be released from its hold. While this dichotomy was apparent in both the religious and philosophical traditions, in both, too, the destiny of men was largely understood as cured through the disciplined, contemplative affirmations of man; that is, by what the ancients knew as *gnosis*. That approach did not deny the disclosure of God, but, through a ladder of ascent, it created forms of understanding in which the divine was characterized as "intellectual." The trinitarian battles were concerned with one point, namely, the overcoming of the split between creation and redemption on the basis of revelation rather than *gnosis*. Hence the trinitarian formulation was the monotheistic declaration that the creator was the redeemer and that the redeemer was the creator, and that God was known as both creator and redeemer by the power of his own activity; that is, by the spirit.

The complicated trinitarian history and the protracted debates concerning one and three make sense in that context; but they are incomprehensible when approached in and of themselves. Historically, it is clear that even the words employed changed their meanings. Anyone cognizant of history knows that the word "person" in an earlier period could be used to make distinctions while preserving unity. Subsequently, however, it developed the very polytheistic overtones which the trinitarian conception originally was meant to overcome. When God was delineated with one body and three heads in late medieval art, the monotheistic, unitarian protest against such a polytheistic trinitarianism became inevitable. The emerging unitarian protest never received its due, because the unitarian direction turned into a rationalist theology. Trinitarian debates were themselves viewed with mixed feelings. Since the Reformation battles were not fought at this point, the reformers pioneered no new direction. At critical points they utilized the traditional formulations against their detractors or subverters. Servetus comes to mind. He did not represent a movement, only the threat of one.

While his material is repetitious, Augustine made the most creative use of the trinitarian conception. He, too, utilized the trinitarian formulation as a way of indicating that the unity of things rested in the unity of God. The trinity became the *arche* by which man was rehabilitated in the world and the world itself given meaning in spite of the decay of the empire. For Augustine, all truth breaks into three parts. On different pages of his writings, the three modes or kinds of knowledge are differently delineated. That this is an inconsistency need not concern us, for Augustine did not work from an analysis of what he saw, but from a conviction that what was left of God's truth in the world, was nothing less than a trinitarian split. The vestiges of truth in the world, whether in nature or history, reflected the triune God in a threeness which had lost its unity. It is as if the Christian understanding of God and man transformed everything from its trinitarian split into a triunity resting in the triune God. The fullest and most instructive account of this phase of Augustine's thought is given by Charles Norris Cochrane in his book, *Christianity and Classical Culture*.

The reason for mentioning the trinitarian problem both in the early church and in its significance for Augustine is that they so clearly indicate the monotheistic intention in the trinitarian formula. Since the meaning of the concept of person has changed, we no longer can say "God in three persons" without endless explanation. But when that phraseology was originally used, the philosophical and legal frames of reference did not contain the later concept of personality so responsible for a polytheistic tone.

It is ironic that the trinitarian conception has been rejected by many since the eighteenth century because of its polytheistic overtones, when, in point of fact, the original intention behind the formulation was to safeguard the monotheism of God against the potential polytheistic splits within and around the Christian movement. While Unitarians attacked the later polytheistic overtones, most Christian bodies ignored them or tried to redefine the ingredients of the formula. In the redefinitions, the trinitarian problem became too closely identified either with a description of the life of God in himself, or of the nature of God's revealing activity. Previously the interrelation of these two aspects was central. Both nature and history, creation and redemption, could be discerningly dealt with in their total scope as long as the trinitarian issue covered both the nature of God and his activity.

But when this range of theological facets is covered otherwise than in trinitarian concerns, as is largely the case today, it does not matter whether or not the term trinity is used. It is helpful to say that such and such an issue was formerly expressed in the trinitarian problem. This gives full credit to those who wrestled with the issues in the early church. The early church was not misled; nor did it employ a barbarous terminology. It was vitally involved in the articulation of faith for its time. We need that same vital involvement as the basis for saying what we need to say today.

Both with reference to the historic debates, and in the light of what has been said about the issues which came to expression in the trinitarian formulations, it is apparent why the trinitarian issues raise the christological ones and why, in turn, the christological ones always raise the trinitarian issues. Simply put, one can say that the declaration that the ground of creation has been made manifest in its redemptive, personal form in Jesus Christ, inevitably raises the whole range of issues.

Within the early church, the christological terms employed were ontological categories, designed both to express and to safeguard the revealing, redemptive activity discerned in Christ. The debates served their purpose. But when victory had been won, the terms were dealt with in isolation from their intention and the debate centered on the acceptance or rejection of the formulations, just as had happened with the trinitarian formulations. This development produced a split between those who insisted upon the traditional formulations without regard for their original setting and those who saw in Jesus of Nazareth simply the declaration of the best of humanity or of a human being who had the most adequate relation to the divine. Today we might more adequately say that in Jesus of Nazareth God has made clear who he is and what we are meant to be, and how, in the light of who he is and what we are meant to be, we might live. We know, then, who God is, who we are, and what we are to become and how that might be accomplished. In that way we can speak of Jesus Christ as both God and man, and in that sense all theology is centered in Jesus Christ as the revelation of God, who is also the revelation of himself to ourselves.

But that formula needs more precise elaboration. In Jesus of Nazareth, the transcendent personal ground of our existence has become manifest. The transcendent dimensions are so clear that the description of Godhead, while borrowed from the language of the early centuries, becomes intelligible. The mystery manifest in him is so distinct from anything which we know or have come to know that he is unique. The debate whether or not such a distinction is one of degree or of kind is not helpful. The actuality of the difference impresses itself upon one. This recognition shows an adoptionist christology to be wrong, however defensible it is against crude theories of incarnation; it makes concepts of preexistence theologically intelligible, while raising questions about the metaphysics of incarnation.

The virgin birth tradition too has meaning in this kind of setting. While the original orientation was to affirm the humanity of Jesus by confirming his birth through a virgin, the divine actuality is simultaneously assumed. Regrettably, the latter subsequently became the major focus of attention. The virgin birth tradition is further complicated by the fact that the Old Testament term translated as virgin meant a woman of marriageable age. An issue arises only when the intentionality of the concept is identified with the categories of biology. Insistence upon the biological virgin birth as a theological axiom is blasphemous, for it makes a biological matter bear a transcendent meaning which it cannot possibly carry. It says both too much and too little.

The symbols which we have mentioned, as well as others in biblical literature, testify to a transcendent presence which is discerned to be nothing less than the divine presence itself. The fullness of that presence becomes the prototype of man's hope. But this fullness is not to be equated with fullness in the sense of the greatness of his humanity. The traditional designa-

131

tion, fully God and fully man, is subject to misunderstanding, for the psychological thrust behind this terminology has been to make both great. The transcendence of God is not its obvious greatness, but its being discerned as great. The full humanity of Jesus is not to be understood in the sense that he is a great man. Indeed, one could probably make the case that there is no such evidence. We operate with a stereotype about the greatness of his being. Contrasted to the great heroes of history, the limitations of his humanity become apparent. It is as if his full humanity had a transparent grandeur, precisely in such a way that the details of his life would keep us from confusing the best of humanity with divinity. The experiences of this man were limited. In his own life, marriage, statecraft, and organization did not exist. He lost his temper and was tempted. Only in suffering and in his being "ungreat" did the lineaments of humanity shine forth in greatness. This greatness showed the marks of his being borne by the transcendent ground.

Just as his life did not encompass many of the facets which men ordinarily experience, so the teachings and declarations which he made are limited to the experiences which he had. Those who have tried to build a theory of ethics out of the sayings of Jesus are hard put to find a comprehensive enough list for all the facets of life. The old question, "What would Jesus do?" is a mistaken attempt to make up for the lack of examples. The question reflects an extrapolating intention. But the teachings of Jesus belong to the context of his life and its implications. That there are not enough teachings to go around should tell us that the emphasis lies elsewhere. Given his life, the teachings are appropriate. They belong together and that should be significant for us.

It is as if the divine presence was fully present in a full humanity, but a humanity which expressed itself in very limited circumstances and situations. The life of Jesus always shows its transparent ground and how life in that sense was meant to be, even though his life occasionally borders on denying it. In Jesus of Nazareth, humanity serves its ground and thereby is a sign to others. Transcendence is present in the fragility of our existence and our humanity. Indeed, this is the setting in which the imitation of Christ becomes significant. It is not the imitation of his noble humanity, but the bearing of the divine mercy in the brokenness of full humanity. That is why Jesus of Nazareth can be seen to have been full of grace and truth.

Along with the ancients, we can say, "fully God, fully man," or, who God is and what we are meant to be. Never has that been so clearly shown forth in a life, and that recognition makes the person of Jesus Christ unique. The limitations of his life, which we noted above, should not blind us but rather help us see the full meaning of its concreteness, of the way in which grace is shown forth at all the concrete junctures of his existence. Without that concreteness, his life could only be an abstract moral example; without that concreteness, his life might also be mistakenly understood as the manifestation of another divine realm, of a God stalking on the earth. But his life is to be understood as the divine presence in all its gracious glory. That is why his life is an analogue, not something to be directly imitated or followed. The transcendent presence is reflected in the concrete situations and decisions. In this sense one can speak of Jesus as the man of faith who is the ground of faith. The detailed picture of his life is essential. Its very concreteness keeps

133

us from that abstraction in which life is the embodiment of ideas and principles rather than life and actuality itself.

One can say that in him life is teaching and doctrine. This is not to be understood as life against teaching or doctrine, or as if his life were an illustration of either. Rather, his life concretely embodied teaching. In exploring his life, the teaching is present; and in exploring the teaching, the life is uniquely present.

His life and what his life declares are one. Hence, he is the expression of the graciousness of God in his own life and the basis from which stem the possibility and meaning of the proclamation of grace. The word, addressed to us as the word of deliverance from ourselves, is the actuality which was present in him, though now it is no longer here in the flesh. Who he was and what he was meant to be is now continued in the proclamation and teaching of the church. That is why his life and message both are recalled, told again. They are living memories which, by the spirit crying unto our spirit, can again become the source of life and lively presence.

Now that he is no longer present in the flesh, the analogue of that fleshliness is given in the sacramental conceptions and realities. This was the rightful instinct among those who declared the sacramental realities, tied in this sense to the church, to be the extension of the incarnation. That viewpoint became a problem when the sacramental realities were made more central than proclamation, and consequent ontological conceptions of the church and its life were developed to buttress and give expression to their viewpoint. But word and sacrament belong together; they are the modes by which that which was once known in the flesh is now known unto us. It is as if God were addressing himself to all our sensibilities. We see the picture of Jesus Christ in the New Testament. We hear the word addressed to us. We taste and know how good the Lord is.

One can show that some of the distortions of the church are related to the overaccenting of one of these facts. The sectarian groups which grew out of the Reformation, as well as sectarian groups within Catholicism, stressed the role of seeing the picture of Jesus and of its imitation; classical Reformation churches overstressed the role of proclamation and of hearing; while the Catholic tradition overstressed the sacramental eating.

The church has had a right instinct in using the analogy of love as the analogy of the divine presence. Fully understood, it includes all the sensibilities of man. But love, too, suffers the distortions for which it was meant to be an appropriate analogy. Love can be declared abstractly and indeed it is; but it reaches its full reality only when it is the love for a concrete human being —that man, that woman. All the declarations of love would be meaningless if love were not made. Truly such a full scope of the meaning of love can be the analogy to word and sacrament.

The Reformation, at its best, understood the relation of word and sacrament. The reformers knew that one could not believe without having heard. In this sense we are formed by hearing and by the comprehension which the ancients referred to as the intellect. But the *doxa* and praise and actuality of God's presence is discerned as known in and through the things of creation. Neither word nor things disclose in and by themselves. They are the media through which the transparent presence of God may be known. It is in that sense that the declaration of love to a woman is cheap and one can escape the giving, sacrificing grandeur of participation. But to make love without the meaning of the word is to be profane, that is, to leave it at the level of biological possibilities or to immerse one's self in mystery and darkness instead of knowing that combination of meaning and mystery which illumines.

Word and sacrament are like that, each needing the other, and the movement from one to the other depends upon the possibilities and dangers. Those who talk too much, whose existence is verbal, need to stress the mystery in life and existence. Those who immerse themselves in the mystery need the clarifying power of the word. The biblical imagery mixes all the levels with a deliberateness that is more than a mixed metaphor, as, for example, "having the eyes of your hearts enlightened" (Eph. 1:18), and "O taste and see that the Lord is good" (Ps. 34:8). The presence of God in its fullness includes the sacramental.

The traditional theories of the atonement must be understood with the same concreteness. They are not statements about the way in which God's deliverance must be understood for all time. It is a mistaken notion to look for a normative theory of the atonement, for it runs counter to the very concreteness of the life and message of Jesus Christ. It is because men experience redemption in terms of the concrete forms of their own need for redemption that the theories are so diverse. The notion of redemption from cosmic powers and forces of evil expresses the ancient world's way of understanding redemption as the direct personal release from such powers; the theory of satisfaction had to do with social structures in which relations of lords and serfs in large part played their roles; the so-called moral influence theory of the atonement was developed in a social context in which to be incorporated into the actuality of love made manifest seemed a realizable, teleological direction. It is not by accident that in our own day we experience redemption as deliverance from meaninglessness, anxieties, despair, loneliness, frustration, etc. But it is also clear that other concerns are already emerging.

If the truth of God meets us concretely, just as it met us concretely in Christ—how could it be otherwise or why should it be otherwise? The significance of these theories may well be that they remind us that facets which we do not directly experience are insights which we ought to consider, because they, too, belong to the full facets of our potential humanity.

2. Accrediting the Foundations

Within the western Christian tradition, two modes of accrediting the significance of Jesus Christ received particular attention —miracle and prophecy. Both the defense of, and attack upon, Christian understanding in the seventeenth and eighteenth centuries centered in these two areas. While significant in the early church, neither miracle nor prophecy received the central attention which succeeding ages gave to them. Sensing the role which they were already beginning to play, but being unwilling to grant them central status, Calvin spoke of both miracle and prophecy as lesser confirmations of faith. It is significant that the reformed tradition misinterpreted Calvin and used him in its own defense of miracle and prophecy.

There was nothing unique about miracles in the early church. In a world in which the distinction was between the ordinary and the extraordinary, rather than between an ordered world and that which breaks the order, extraordinary events and happenings were simply assumed. Indeed, it is remarkable that the Christian movement played down the role of miracles, for its interest in miracles was less pronounced than that of the contemporary pagan sects. Moreover, miracles were never interpreted in isolation from their setting. Demons, powers, magicians were not refuted by their being extraordinary in the early church, but by the relation of the miraculous to what was taught, called "the teaching." The fact of extraordinary power was assumed everywhere; the real problem centered in the kind of extraordinary power involved. Hence, the correlation of miracle and teaching was natural to Christians.

The "teaching," which for the early church meant its message about life and meaning, certainly was considered to have transcendent foundations. And only the miracles which were appropriate to the teaching could be utilized to accredit such foundations. To do so, the early church distinguished between miracles which were credible and those which were incredible. A miracle could only be a credible sign in an appropriate context of understanding and meaning. When utilized along with other signs and expectations, miracles helped to give credibility to Christian understanding.

It was a change of the first order when seventeenth-century dogmaticians singled out miracles in and by themselves as proof of Christian truth. In a situation in which the world was increasingly understood as a spectacle of order, these theologians understood that transcendent dimensions were being pushed to the side and needed defense. But a direct defense of such dimensions by accentuating that miracles did happen, or had happened, was of dubious value. Isolated from their context, miracles could only be approached as an issue of feasibility, of whether or not they occurred. That was a mislocated line of defense.

In a world which does not accept either the cosmological possibilities of the early church or the invasion of the natural by the supernatural, other ways to express what miracle means must be found. We have indicated that faith, or being a believer, is a mystery. Rejecting the overt conception that miracle is an invasion of the natural order, Schleiermacher at the beginning of the nineteenth century declared "all" is miracle. The more religious you are the more does everything become miracle, for miracle is the religious name for natural event. Others, such as Rauschenbusch, understood the transformation of personal life as miracle. All such statements identify miracle with faith. But for most of Christian history the term has meant more than that.

In the early centuries miracles had been considered accompanying signs, that is, visible signs, anchored in and based upon another reality. In a world in which such signs were less evident, some seventeenth- and eighteenth-century critics and friends alike concluded that miracles, which had occurred in the past in order to attest a teaching or a person, had ceased long ago, and that they were no longer necessary. A more invidious attack came from those who declared that such miracle stories were deliberately fabricated, or fabricated out of inadequate evidence.

Originally, miracles corroborated faith, but by the seventeenth century, corroboration already had become proof. That shift entirely changed the meaning of miracles, for they were no longer understood in faith but as the basis for faith. Indeed, miracles do not establish faith, or at least it is dangerous when they are so conceived. What God allegedly has done then becomes a graceless point of attention, pointing to itself rather than beyond itself.

Miracle may be defined as faith comprehending deliverance at a nexus of nature and destiny. The role of psychosomatic factors and the mystery of deliverance from incurable disease may be analogous to, or identifiable with, the conception of miracle. Such occurrence may certainly be understood as miracles by the believer, though such miracles are more properly appropriated in silence than in too much talk about them. Declarations turn faith into magic. A believing quizzicalness is germane to miracle.

A concatenation of events in which nature and history intermesh is the second form of what has come to be known as miracle. The deliverance from Egypt is a major example. Indeed, deliverance is the miracle. The parting of the waters of the Red Sea or the wind blowing them back are the subsidiary apprehensions surrounding the central act of deliverance. It is as if the greatness of what has occurred is attested by the subsidiary, miraculous stories which emerged. Stories including miraculous facets have been associated with all the great events and figures of history.

Miracle is an appropriate word for the special redemptive appearances which faith discerns at the concatenation of factors where nature and destiny coincide. Miracles make believers gasp by the special unexpected presence of the divine. Faith makes a difference, but the difference which faith makes is related to the total surrounding circumstances, not to the manipulative powers behind them. Faith itself is greater than any miracle, or so it was understood until miracles became the proof of faith. Miracles, like the accenting of individual scriptural passages, must be suppressed, so that they may return to their rightful setting. When so pushed down, they are not to be despised but can again take on their appropriate role.

A similar accrediting role was evident in the conception of prophecy. In discussing prophecy, it is also necessary immediately to distinguish the world in which the conception arose and operated from the reality expressed through it. Until the eighteenth century, it was largely assumed that the past determines the future. Hence, the future could be predicted, if one found the adequate key. But the context in which the early church understood prophecy was that the expectations of God had been fulfilled and that therefore one could, in looking back, establish the appropriate connections.

It was not unusual for secular documents to be used to define and to divine what would happen in the future. This was part of the fabric of common understanding, and even the myths of Homer were used in attempts to predict the future. It was not unnatural, then, for Christians to claim that the Messiah who had been expected as the predicted one had come, and that one could see that the signs had been fulfilled. But the emphasis was always on the expectations which had been fulfilled. Christians could more significantly claim that the past had been validated and expectations fulfilled by documenting and proof texting out of the history of Israel, than could those who claimed that the writings of Homer had been validated in the political realities of the empire. The actual advantage of scripture so used inevitably made the argument more significant than it should have become, and subsequently triggered the defense at the wrong point.

That the predictions had been fulfilled served well as a

continuing sign in a context in which the assumption was that the past determined the future, and in which truth was already present, needing only to be uncovered. But the seventeenth century utilized prophecy in a sheerly predictive mode as a direct, simple way of authenticating Christian truth against all on-comers. It indulged in the exercise of trying to show how an Old Testament passage actually predicted the future in detail, and it rejoiced when a passage of great antiquity could be found whose predictive power had come true. Therefore Moses was preferred over Isaiah, for the length of time between the prediction and its fulfillment could be extended. In this same way, the determination of all things by God now became, not the way in which history had meaning as in Luther or Calvin, but the oppressive category by which all freedom and spontaneity in the world were expunged through the determination of the hidden hand of God. The powerful hold of this seventeenth-century approach is still blatantly present in fundamentalist groups who use scripture in this fashion; it played a demonic role in the formation and continuation of antisemitism in the church by its continued use of Old Testament texts in this predictive, determined fashion.

The working assumption in this way of thinking is that the prophets prophesy the future. It was thought that the dire visions and allusions of the prophets, which the initiated contemporaries understood as having reference to events in their own time, contained hidden clues about the future. So the successors of the prophets made reference to the world empires of the future. The four monarchies of the Book of Daniel were invariably used in later periods as a kind of divining instrument about coming political developments usually having to do with the end of the world.

In revulsion to the playing of such mathematical games with the biblical texts, the notion also arose at a later time that prophecy had to do with what a prophet did in another way, namely, to forthtell. But this was a somewhat simpleminded, pious response rather than a hardheaded one.

Instead, the prophet's role can be said to lay bare the pretensions of ages and periods. The lineaments of that task always demand the articulation of the consequences. The prophet has the strange role of being theologically right, but of being usually wrong on details or consequences. That is because history is both more complex and more subject to unanticipated factors which redirect it, than the prophet imagines or sees. With a seering, single-minded intent, the prophet sees what he sees. That he is wrong in detail does not invalidate the burden of the message. Indeed, in details the biblical prophets were hardly ever right. That is why fundamentalists have such a hard time, for they have to interpret texts in other than their known meaning in order to establish the connections which are necessary for their theory.

3. *Extrapolating the Foundations*

If miracle and prophecy can be understood as accrediting the foundations, the concepts of predestination and providence can be said to be an exercise in extrapolating the foundations. In both modes faith confesses its anchorage in the divine.

In the early church, the powers of fate and fortune were experienced as oppressive forces which had to be overcome. And strange as it sounds to our ears, this occurred both by a deterministic view of predestination and by an emphasis upon the significance of human decision, to an extent later described as Pelagian. To be determined by God and to affirm the significance of human, moral, and religious decision, contradictory as they seem, together refuted the determination of the dark powers of fate, and by definition the unanticipated events of fortune. It was Augustine who first did battle both against fate and fortune, and against a Pelagian conception of man. For him, the deterministic development of predestination was a fruitful weapon against both fate and Pelagianism.

Even the Reformation conception of predestination still operated fundamentally in a deterministic framework. The power of deterministic modes of thinking had come to take a new instinctive hold on the minds of men in the Reformation period. Indeed, the ancient powers of fate and fortune were felt with fresh power. In philosophy, the rebirth of atomism at this time buttressed the double motifs of fate and fortune, that is, an ineluctable fate integrally related to a chance combination of atoms. Moreover, Calvin, like Augustine, utilized a deterministic view as a final weapon against what he considered the new Pelagianism, that is, medieval work-righteousness. As a last recourse, he argued that if destiny is completely determined by God, all claims of accomplishment, including those in grace, count for naught.

But even such an argument, as well as the broad approach we have been describing for the first fifteen centuries of Christian history, must be seen in its total setting. This includes two significant points. First, and as already indicated, within the deterministic context the argument essentially is that determination by God is meaningful over against purposeless and arbitrary determination. It is hard for us to realize that on the basis of God's determination, for the first time history was considered dependable and safe. History was within the pale of God's trustworthy activity. Today's question, whether history is open, was barely on the horizon of consciousness. The question then was whether the decreed events of life and history could be meaningful. In that setting the determination by God was the light that shone in the darkness caused by experienced, oppressive powers.

Second, while the deterministic outlook was accepted, it was not in fact the point of departure for theological understanding. Theology was still faith seeking understanding and doing battle with alternative positions. It was not by accident that Calvin elaborated his concept of predestination in the section on faith, and that in the light of his logic of faith, double predestination, in spite of certain explicit passages of scripture, was considered to be the obverse implication of predestination. This was a tacit admission that predestination was the more significant, because it alone was known in faith. It was a similar viewing of predestination in the context of faith which finally led Luther virtually to abandon the concept of double predestination.

For Luther and for Calvin, predestination means essentially the believer's confessing and affirming that the mystery of faith is grounded in the mystery of God's electing, communicating activity. But it is only in faith that this confession is made, and reflection about it apart from faith is considered prying and entering into caverns of abstract speculation. On that path, they contended, one stood either before an absurdity or an abyss of terror. For them, predestination in the setting of faith meant that predestination was at once meaningful and a tremendous comfort. While predestination was known only in the light of faith, to trust the destiny which God had in part disclosed in this gift and miracle was a comfort in the midst of any wavering or uncertainty in faith. Calvin, contrary to the stereotype of those who either do not read him or choose to misread him, called upon believers to trust their predestination, to see and accept its comfort and security in the struggle of life and of faith.

Succinctly, it can be said that with reference to the general deterministic views of life, the reformers stressed the all-working and determining character of God; with reference to the mystery of faith, they stressed the trustworthy destiny of God. But in both instances, the delineation of predestination was formed by faith. In the first case the deterministic categories are shared by believers and nonbelievers alike. In the second, the deterministic categories are subsumed under the more appropriate term correlative to faith, such as mystery, destiny, dependability, and trust. Hence, the deterministic categories abound when they are shared as a part of the world view of the time; they are comparatively sidetracked when the distinctly theological problems of faith and destiny are developed.

But in the Renaissance-Reformation period one also has the beginnings of strong protests against deterministic ways of thinking. The attack of Erasmus upon Luther's position was more than the traditional semi-Pelagian caveat against the rigorous and vigorous defenders of grace alone. It was also the burst of the Renaissance stress upon the natural powers of man against the powers of darkness, namely, the dark powers of nature and history. In that situation, the reformers stressed God's control over all things while the Renaissance forged new directions and by their

God-given power challenged the older conceptions of darkness and man's depravity. To the more traditional thinkers, this stress upon the new powers of man threatened the theological accenting of the power of God, and they considered the stress upon such power as deprived from God, at best, as a cover-up of the true situation. From the perspective of the present, it is not possible to deny that the natural powers of man, even when their source was ascribed to God, were determinative for the realms of faith, history, and redemption. The Enlightenment was the logical conclusion of this development.

While the more orthodox churchmen, as we have indicated, did believe that the power of reason was adequate for the natural knowledge of God, they vigorously rejected the power of man in matters of faith and redemption. In fact, instead of confessing the mystery of the inception of faith while affirming the priority of God's activity as the ground and foundation of response, the orthodox theologians now utilized deterministic categories to defend and guarantee the origin and nature of faith. In reaction to Renaissance confidence, they developed misguided deterministic views on predestination. The dubious use of deterministic categories in defense of faith, already present in Calvin though not for the origin and essential nature of faith, became the point of departure for the orthodox Protestant thinkers. God had determined who would have faith and who would not. In this transition, the understanding of the issues was transposed. Now abstract discussions and debates concerning predestination were inevitable. Faith no longer was the context for predestination; rather, predestination understood as the determined, decreed plan of God for everyone was the guarantee of faith. It hardly mattered whether the contention was that such decrees had reference primarily to the elect or to the nonelect as well; it mattered even less whether they were anchored in the secret determination of each individual's destiny beyond all reference to the fall, as in supralapsarian views, or with reference to the fall, as in infralapsarian views. In each instance, an abstract determinism was the foundation of faith. And this development occurred at the precise juncture in history when deterministic modes were drastically being challenged in the birth pangs of the modern world.

In contrast, Luther and Calvin both had been so careful in the grounding of predestination and had used deterministic categories only when they belonged to the generally accepted way of thinking. It is significant that they shied away from deterministic categories as much as they did in matters of faith. But in the light of the subsequent orthodox development, it was almost inevitable that among the successors to the orthodox theologians, predestination should be transformed into a general decree, the details of which were filled in by each man's own decision, as in the Arminian turning of a bad thing to Pelagian advantage; or that the concept of predestination should be rejected entirely, as among those who simply reacted against the older views. It is surely one of the best proofs of the sociological transmission of unexamined knowledge that the man on the street, even if he has rejected the entire Christian heritage or stands vaguely but positively within it, defines predestination as the conviction that all details concerning the faith and destiny of every man have been determined by God.

As predestination affirmed God's trustworthiness with respect to individual existence, so providence expressed this trustworthiness for collective life in nature and in history. And just as providence, in analogy to predestination, once had as its mode of expression the past projecting and predicting the future, so now it must be understood as God's presence at the junctures where the concatenations of life and historical existence open new possibilities. There is no need then to delineate the historical development of the concept of providence, for it bears direct analogy to the history of predestination. And in both instances, we must now be ready for the openness of the future. While the past carries its burden and its determining modes into our existence, it is also true that for most of us the world is considered open toward the future.

Thus one of the great transformations in historical understanding occurred in the eighteenth century when it was no longer believed that the past either did or ought to determine the future, and when it was felt instead that the future was open for man to determine and develop. In that new-won power, men frequently understood the openness of the future as if they were themselves creating history along deterministic patterns, that now they, rather than God or alien powers, were determining the future. But the openness of history means precisely that there is no process by which it can be determined or directly understood, though it may be illumined. Social forces, cultural or theological developments, men of vision with insight and charisma—all these are present in history, and the relations and formative powers are never exhausted by the factors which seem to be in them. Perhaps that is why Paul spoke of wrestling, not with flesh and blood, but with principalities and powers. We discern the ingredients which form history, but we are confronted by the tantalizingly open, unknown future.

The concepts of predestination and providence may today

be understood as the way in which faith extrapolates its foundations in order to encompass the mystery of its own faith and to affirm the safety of the unknown future. Predestination may still be the confession of the believer that he can comprehend his faith only as the gift which God destined for him; but as a believer he must strictly confine that conception to his own confessional boundaries. Providence may be the confession of the believer that the world is safely in the hands of God even though it is open to unheard-of possibilities of good and evil.

VII

EMERGING CONTOURS

1. Analogies for Theology

In the preceding chapters considerable attention has been given to the reasons why theology, as we have known it, cannot simply be continued as in the past. This does not imply a negative judgment on theology, but rather that we must take seriously that there may be many modes which theology might take in order to be faithful to its task. It has been suggested, too, that simply abandoning the older theologies will not do, because they continue to exercise an insidious role. Moreover, their positive contributions must be appropriated by penetrating into the intentionality behind them. Attention has also been given to the way in which such intentionality might begin to be expressed in modes more congenial to our current universes of discourse.

But this is only a beginning. There are signs that theology, as the church, is beckoned to a more drastic abandonment of its traditionally recognized forms than has been suggested here. Theological work and thought in the future may not look like anything we have recognized as theology before. Indeed, theology may have to become nontheology, just as much art has become nonart. This leaves open the question, as it does in art, whether it is theology at all—and how shall we know? We shall not. A world is being born and the risk is that we shall stand outside it, or that we shall be too much a part of it. But the courage and risk it demands of us cannot be avoided. Faith includes the risk that we, who may be wrong, nevertheless will serve the future and be justified in our faltering attempts. But the temptation for many is to seek safety in a repetition of the past or to make a commitment to one or two of the strident movements vaguely articulating the unaccustomed ways of sensing things.

For some, what is here accepted will mean that the *logos* of theology has disappeared, that theology has come to an end. But not all form need have the form of the older *logos*. The new emerging forms are strange to the eye and to the ear, and for many they appear as if they had no form at all. Some of the new is formless, decadent, and chaotic. But much of it represents affirmations and styles as valid as anything that has yet appeared in creation. There is an obvious wastefulness in history, hard for those who do not live by grace to accept, much less to comprehend. It is as if God tolerated such waste more than we do. He has warned all theological do-gooders to keep hands off, lest they tear up the tares with the wheat.

It has been suggested that these new forms are emerging in literature, in the arts, and in historical understanding, more belatedly in the social sciences and in the philosophical disciplines. Certainly, no new philosophical impulse, understanding metaphysics in terms of dynamics, has emerged upon the scene. There are hopeful signs among those theologians who are trying to take seriously the philosophy of Whitehead and Heidegger, like John Cobb, Jr., and Schubert Ogden.

Theology in any case has not yet made any of the major transitions to new shapes as, e.g., is evident in the arts. The radical historicity of all creation may be evident in the deliberate use by some contemporary artists of materials which will not survive, and therefore make their art come to an end. And such approaches are taken by artists of exceptional competence, whose work is not ephemeral. One can also say that major changes have occurred among artists of great discipline and training, whose work is indeed meant to survive. Jackson Pollock and Barnett Newman will stand in the grand tradition of art. They may or may not survive as a Rembrandt or a Picasso have survived, and even about the latter, there are vacillations of judgment. But all these men share a common technical competence. Looking at them may provide interesting clues for changing modes of apprehending reality.

There is a greater affinity between Rembrandt and Picasso than between a painting by Picasso and a painting by Jackson Pollock. There is a connection between Rembrandt and Picasso in that the traditional forms and the ways of conceiving things are still evident. The same techniques and forms are found in both. Picasso's art does not break through the traditional ways of seeing. No new art forms emerged with him; the old forms are still apparent, and the attempt to say something new has been conveyed through distortion, deflection, and disarray. There is an annihilation of bits but not a transformation of the whole. Seventeenth-century theology is like Rembrandt—though I like Rembrandt considerably more than seventeenth-century theology —and Tillich is like Picasso. Indeed, connecting Tillich and Picasso has its own justification through Tillich's insinuation of his views concerning Picasso's *Guernica* into the theological discourse of the modern world.

When one comes to a man like Jackson Pollock, the situation is entirely different. The traditional forms have disappeared. The boundaries do not exist. In music, too, even Stravinsky is like the great classical composers of the past. It is with the music of composers like John Cage that the traditional forms have disappeared. The usual boundaries do not exist, and the contours of things are no longer traditional. The new gropings are not without their form, nor without their formative power. But the new form is not yet recognizable or, if so, is not yet one to which we are accustomed. Today there is a randomness which bespeaks life itself with its contours of meaning and of dynamics. We live in a waiting, forming period. The expressions of faith and thought must utilize the vitality of new forms strange to our eyes and to our hearing, hardly familiar or lasting, but somehow speaking in and to our time.

If we are going to take this step we shall not be so comprehensive as a Tillich or so discursive as a Barth, nor so concerned as the existentialists to be right about so little, even if it is so central. The contours of faith are as open, as imaginative and dynamic, as the promise and perils of this age. We need a perspective that does not arrest the future or repeat the past, but rather reflects the courage and grace to meet the uncertain dynamics of this time. Then the cultural concerns may meet and form new constellations as discerned and wrestled with in faith. By definition, this approach will not provide a theology for all time. But such readiness of faith and diligent work may open us to what the eye has not seen or ear has not heard.

A theology so born can resist the temptation toward absolute form or toward absolute formlessness. In such a dawning time, the issues cannot be forced. It is, therefore, a working, waiting time; and it does not matter whether the time is short or long.

Theology, in this sense, is always concrete. A few insights are better than general truths which do not touch reality. The concrete theologies of the past had powerful things to say to their own times. And the comparatively undated theologies of the past say little to our time; perhaps they too said more to their times. Surely Reinhold Niebuhr will be one of the most dated theologians in history. But anyone who has lived in his presence or witnessed the theological scene in America will know the role which such theological work has played. By contrast, Tillich will be more timeless. However, if one asks the question of the source of the decisive change in American theology in the first half of the twentieth century, one would unambiguously have to reply Niebuhr rather than Tillich. The different gifts of men play their part in diverse ways. In a theological community the interests and concerns are complimentary, even when contradictory. They serve the totality of faith.

A new diversity is entering into theological work. Within the theological community no one can any longer be equally at home in all the facets of theology, much less the systematic discipline the theologian once thought he must unify. While a vision of the whole may be a human longing, no one can any longer create a unified system of any major significance. Theology will demand teamwork or the sharing of theological labors, where scholars learn from one another and gladly accept the enriching fruits of the labors of others. There will be specialties in the theological domain, where people with particular competencies work on particular issues, perhaps relevant secular issues or disciplines.

There is nothing wrong with a specialist as such. The problem arises when the specialist has no wider concerns than what he is doing and is not interested in how the facets of what he is about relate to the facets of contiguous areas. Indeed, such contiguousness and intersecting of individual concerns has frequently become the basis for the creation of new fields. The creation of such new disciplines reflects the human and scholarly concern for more adequate approaches to knowledge. This kind of competence, which seeks its equality and relation to other areas with a due sense of the limitations it imposes on all, is to be preferred to the overarching schemes of unity and of comprehension which violate what people do know.

In scholarly and theological worlds generally, each person is still considered to be his own master. Hardly anyone accepts the conclusions of others without testing them himself. Scholarly teamwork in research and teaching is only at its threshold. The old adage of "going it alone" or "building the theory oneself" is still deeply ingrained in those in academic life. But the interrelating of facets of knowledge and of truth will demand a common enterprise. What one can know onself may be most real. But it is also limited and hence must be opened by the horizons and concerns of others.

2. *An Emerging Humanity*

The new ways of understanding are not only new modes. They exhibit reality in a new way. The older ways of seeing reality cannot be declared so much right or wrong as no longer viable. The new way of seeing reality may still have an identity with the old; but it may look entirely different. It may be a facet of reality that has been neglected before or which has not been seen that way before. So it can be said that history both deprives and enriches us.

The close relation between the changing modes of apprehension and reality itself raises the question whether or not there is such a thing as constancy in human nature. Is there, for instance, an eternal law upon which man reflects and which is reflected in him? It appears as if the very conception of a stable or unchanging nature is modeled upon an older conception of nature and belongs to a part of that fixed structure and putting everything in its place which contemporary modes reject. Whether man reflects the natural law of God, as in the older theologies, or the moral law within, as in Kant, man is defined by an identifiable structure which ties himself, the world, and God together. In these traditions, man could be called a rational animal, because the function of reason tied all these ingredients together. Reasoning was the expression of the totality of a structure of reason and of order.

It is small wonder that a decay of this intellectual structure from the eighteenth century on has been understood by many as the decay of the moral order as well. Indeed, from the perspective of those who approach the issue from such an orientation, the conclusions follow as night follows day. But it does not necessarily follow that morality is threatened; it only follows that the particular conception of what is considered moral has lost its hold. It is just as plausible to suggest that another conception of morality is taking its place.

That differences of world views do define the moral order

is evident in the generation gap, which is more acute at this juncture of history than at any past time of which we have knowledge. Since those who represent the new emerging styles are so acutely aware that the apprehension of reality and its living form must coincide, they attack the alleged pretense of their elders, who quite frankly accepted the split between the two. For western history, the moral nature of man defined ideal being, what man essentially was, and how that related to ultimate reality. The gap between the ideal and the actual situations was accepted, because it was assumed that man's aberrations were distorting to, but not destructive of, his essential nature. The devastating eruptions of our history and an existentialist, intellectual response has led many to say that reality is truly only where man lives. The ideal self has no personal or ontological validity. Man is what man sees and does.

Given these diverse orientations, it is natural that the young should say that anyone over thirty is not to be trusted. But those who say this do not see how much their own orientation to existence is simply drawing different conclusions about a problem they have not reconceived. The new generation is as concerned as the old to be right and true; but rather than projecting the right in terms of that which is to be but is not now, it defines all problems by limiting the horizons so that they can be managed. The new generation shares the existentialist impulse to be right even if it means that one needs to bracket out so much that is complex and does not fit. From sex to politics, the new generation rejects what it has been taught, and to its elders it looks as if all structure has been abandoned. But it is so moral in the sex it practices and the politics it eschews, that it flaunts its virtue and would create a world devoid of nuance, complexity, and color. Its power may well lie in creating a climate in which the unacknowledged structural contradictions in our society will collapse. Out of that climate more viable forms of life may yet emerge for all. But it will not happen without much agony.

But there are horizons of new orientations being born in the most unexpected quarter. In the intellectual community, it is widely assumed that the technological revolution is the enemy of humanity. Indeed, in a technological society, quantitative analysis and thus controlling possibilities do present themselves. Even surveys, which depend upon quantification, raise the question of how much they predict and to what extent they influence what they predict. They leave leadership out of account and unexpected factors occasionally alter everything.

Let us take the computer as an illustration. While it provides limited solutions, it makes us more aware of the complexity of problems and of the endless array of problems. The computer can simultaneously handle so many ingredients that the mind of man is dwarfed by comparison. But that limited extension of the brain raises new problems and possibilities. It lays little to rest and opens more vistas than it closes. Rather, the technological age, as symbolized in the computer, makes man problem-centered. Man is becoming accustomed to the fact that he has problems and that the nature of his very life is to be dealing with them continually.

Our heritage has encouraged us to believe that problems need and can be solved once and for all. That this is so deep in our bones is related to our intellectual history. The United States is related both to the residue of seventeenth-century thought, in which everything must have its rightful place and a solution as well, and to the pragmatic American temperament, which is devoted to finding solutions. But what the technological age has made clear—and, on another level as well, the political order— is that man is not so much a rational animal as a problem-addressing animal. The new man born of the technological revolution is a person who sees problems as possibilities, and his life is lived in shifting seas in which directions are competently being changed but remain open to redirection at any time. Perhaps this is why the establishment and the young generation who stand against the establishment alike attack this type of man. They would both like to be certain; they are opposite sides of the same coin.

It is at least conceivable that the frank avowal of problems as endless alternative possibilities is nearer to the biblical message than most of the alternatives. One cannot even rightly call this approach problem-solving, for the term problem-solving carries the mark of a "solution" within it. If there are no solutions but only possibilities, a new mode of life and coping with it has been born. Possibilities can be frustrated, helped, left alone. Possibilities are always partially elusive; nor are they susceptible of a single approach as a sole alternative. Indeed, that is why problems are so human and why they call upon man's imagination and experience, both his own and those of the human race.

This type of man is a new kind. He does not think in blacks or whites or even grays. He thinks concretely, with long- and short-range possibilities ever before him. He makes plans, but he is ready to scrap them; and he knows that if he does not plan for the future, he cannot creatively meet what it demands of him.

3. *Theology and Humanity*

The dynamics of man's life create the possibility of unlimited creativity for good and apparently limitless capacity for destruction. Structures of government and of social processes have the double function of facilitating the natural flow of life as its best and of placing limits and checks upon the bent toward destruction. The possibility of destructiveness leads moralists and officialdom alike to stress the authority of ideas and of forms of life at the very moment when disruptiveness is a sign that they no longer serve mankind adequately. This does not mean that, once such an extremity has been reached, the world must be abandoned to anarchy. But it does mean that the time has been reached when dramatic reorientations of outlook and practice are long overdue.

The channeling of the dynamics of man, so that his individual and societal aspects mutually enrich each other, is the object of statecraft. But the best structures are at once the expression of, and the check upon, the power which the dynamics of man engender. The fear of this power has led and continues to lead to ethical shortcuts. The puritan ethos channeled the activity of man as a responsible believer into the productiveness of work as the safest course of action. Hence, Puritans became suspicious of leisure, and the acquisition of goods became a sign of divine favor, for busy people became prosperous. A more liberal but equally moral ethic attacked the passionate nature of man's dynamism and domesticated his hopes and his humanity as a way of keeping him out of trouble. Indeed, it can be said that there are those who, to use the proverbial expression, sin less than others. This is not always so much the virtue of their being, as it is the lack of the courage to live. Society has been so suspicious of the dynamism of man that its ideal is nearer to the vegetative character of plants. Man's capacity for mischief is thereby reduced, but his capacities for creative venturesomeness are alike subdued. To be human is potentially dangerous, as dangerous as the risk of creation itself.

This is why Pascal said that man is neither brute nor angel but man, and hastened to add that he who would act the angel would end by acting the brute. This is also why Luther could say that God's grace is sufficient; therefore sin and sin bravely but, more bravely still, believe. It was not that Luther was looking for sins to commit; rather he recognized that the price of advance includes the price of one's own sin, as well as that the choices and alternatives are seldom as clear-cut as one would like.

Decisions are difficult, precisely because the alternatives are not between right and wrong. One must find the grace to act, for situations given the normal canons of right and wrong would incapacitate one for action. Such dilemmas do not in themselves determine the character of decisions; sometimes it may be necessary to say a decisive "no" to the alternatives. But the complexity and interrelations of factors and people do so circumscribe decisions that one has his own possibility of life and freedom only in grace, not in the correctness of the decision itself.

The church, of all institutions, should know the complexity involved in the problem of justice and the problems inherent in social structures without becoming incapacitated to deal with them. It was fairly late in the church's history that it learned that structures were themselves the expression of love or evil, and that some forms of political order were more adequate than others. For some, this is still hard to accept. But others have come to understand that while the church must talk of love and of changing people's hearts, the church also has to see love expressed in justice, and therefore must encourage the use of political power for creating the context in which people's hearts may be changed; and if that does not happen, it must bring men to act in certain just ways whether or not their hearts be ready.

Church and society generally need to live with more grace than either wishes. For forgiveness will always need to encompass both the wrath of those who strike out when people belatedly help, and to be modest in the presence of achievements whenever they do occur, for such accomplishments can never stand the grandeur ascribed to them.

A faithful orientation to ethical and moral values is one in which the dynamics of grace and of empowering action surround all the facets man needs to take into account. It demands a simplicity of grace, open and enabling, for decisions in multitudinous, contradictory, concrete alternatives. Grace means being able to act without being sure; of doing so because under God one is so placed. Grace means assessing, risking, a human concern which does not think in right or wrong, but in accepting, directing terms. Such an approach is neither squeamish nor ruthless, neither purist nor opportunistic, but gracious, with integrity and compassion. In some sense it can be said to be situational: but it is not a contextual ethic in the usual sense of that term. A contextual ethic usually operates on the basis of absolute norms which it then tries to apply relatively. The orientation here suggested relates grace more directly to the given dynamics of man's historical nature. The norm, as indicated in the previous chapter, is made concrete in Jesus of Nazareth and can operate by analogy. An ethical application, whether by the way of the absolute or of the relative, destroys both the concreteness and the dynamics of life.

Faith, by its nature, includes moral and ethical concerns. But in Christian understanding such concerns do not stand by themselves. When the church talks grace without action, it is a deadly institution. When it talks words and actions without grace, it is pretentious and becomes political. But when it is informed by a comprehending faith, it is at best ready for new forms and is less anxiously concerned about the life-and-death character of alternatives. The church ought to comprehend change better than its secular equivalents. The church particularly, for example, ought to know that the family is no longer the ideal unit it was, that indeed it had its own negative authoritarian side; that our children are formed by factors which we can no longer privately control; that sex is both more and less important, even if misused, than we make it. These factors demand new ethical orientations. They do not demand that we accept the factors as such. But as a minimum necessity the new factors must be included in all reconceptions.

All this means a new thrust, an entering of the church again into all arenas of life—not as a Christian civilization which is in control or enunciates the values, but as an instrument present in the places where things need to be done, in places "where cross the crowded ways of life." Church buildings will be built less often; shared cathedral centers will emerge without traditional church structures. New forms of worship and work will emerge. There are signs that at least a part of the church is moving into the heart of urban issues, into the places where a new moral thrust aimed at the principalities and powers can do untold good. Theological education will change. While the basic contours of faith demand a study of the depths of historical understanding, theological students must be tested, formed, and made professionally competent in the crucible where life is lived.

Only a faithful, energetic reconception of the present task at all levels will do. That demands all the ingredients which have been touched upon—knowing where we have been, knowing where we are, knowing what we have to do. In that enterprise, new forms strange to behold, unaccustomed to the eye or to our responses, will occur. And it may be found that the faith which informed our fathers will find its repetition in an authentic new tradition, the new creations born out of anguish, burning with a simplicity of faith, endlessly wresting with the actual complexities. Then we will be continually on the job as those who have neither the time nor the inclination to be either pessimistic or optimistic. Faith is both more relaxing and more demanding than the definable alternatives usually presented to us.

SELECTED BIBLIOGRAPHY

General Bibliography of Recent Books on New Directions

Altizer, Thomas J. J., and Hamilton, William. *Radical Theology and the Death of God.* Indianapolis: Bobbs-Merrill Company, 1966.
Caponigri, Aloysius, ed. *Modern Catholic Thinkers: An Anthology.* New York: Harper & Row, 1965.
Cobb, John B., Jr. *A Christian Natural Theology: Based on the Thought of Alfred North Whitehead.* Philadelphia: The Westminster Press, 1965.
———. *The Structure of Christian Existence.* Philadelphia: The Westminster Press, 1967.
Ebeling, Gerhard. *God and Word.* Tr. by James Leitch. Philadelphia: Fortress Press, 1967.
———. *The Problem of Historicity in the Church and Its Proclamation.* Tr. by Grover Foley. Philadelphia: Fortress Press, 1967.
———. *Theology and Proclamation: Dialogue with Bultmann.* Tr. by John Riches. Philadelphia: Fortress Press, 1967.
Funk, Robert W. *Language, Hermeneutic, and Word of God.* New York: Harper & Row, 1966.
Gustafson, James M. *Christ and the Moral Life.* New York: Harper & Row, 1968.
Hall, Charles A. M. *The Common Quest: Theology and the Search for Truth.* Philadelphia: The Westminster Press, 1965.
Hartshorne, Charles. *A Natural Theology for Our Time.* La Salle, Ill.: Open Court Publishing Company, 1967.
Hartt, Julian N. *A Christian Critique of American Culture: An Essay in Practical Theology.* New York: Harper & Row, 1967.

166

Harvey, Van A. *The Historian and the Believer: The Morality of Historical Knowledge and Christian Belief*. New York: The Macmillan Company, 1966.

Hazelton, Roger. *Christ and Ourselves: A Clue to Christian Life Today*. New York: Harper & Row, 1965.

———. *A Theological Approach to Art*. Nashville: Abingdon Press, 1967.

High, Dalles M. *Language, Persons, and Belief: Studies in Wittgenstein's Philosophical Investigations and Religious Uses of Language*. New York: Oxford University Press, 1967.

Lonergan, Bernard. *Collection: Papers by Bernard Lonergan*. Ed. by F. E. Crowe. New York: Herder & Herder, 1967.

Macquarrie, John. *God-Talk: An Examination of the Language and Logic of Theology*. New York: Harper & Row, 1967.

———. *Principles of Christian Theology*. New York: Charles Scribner's Sons, 1966.

Maguire, John D. *The Dance of the Pilgrim: A Christian Style of Life for Today*. New York: Association Press, 1967.

Michalson, Carl. *Worldly Theology: The Hermeneutical Focus of an Historical Faith*. New York: Charles Scribner's Sons, 1967.

Moltmann, Jürgen. *Theology of Hope: On the Ground and the Investigations of Christian Eschatology*. Tr. by James Leitch. New York: Harper & Row, 1967.

Ogden, Schubert M. *The Reality of God, and Other Essays*. New York: Harper & Row, 1966.

Outler, Albert C. *Who Trusts in God: Musings on the Meaning of Providence*. New York: Oxford University Press, 1968.

Pannenberg, Wolfhart. *Jesus—God and Man*. Philadelphia: The Westminster Press, 1968.

Rahner, Karl. *Belief Today*. Tr. by M. H. Heelan. New York: Sheed & Ward, 1967.

Reist, Benjamin A. *Toward a Theology of Involvement: The Thought of Ernst Troeltsch*. Philadelphia: The Westminster Press, 1966.

Williams, Daniel Day. *The Spirit and the Forms of Love.* New York: Harper & Row, 1968.

(For additional Roman Catholic literature, the reader is referred particularly to the writings of Gregory Baum, Hans Küng, Bernard Häring, Karl Rahner, Leslie Dewart, and Edward C. F. A. Schillebeeckx.)

New Series in Paper or Hard Book Format

Concilium: Theology in the Age of Renewal. Marcel Vanhengel, executive secretary. Glen Rock, N. J.: Paulist Press.

Journal for Theology and the Church. Ed. Robert W. Funk in association with Gerhard Ebeling. New York: Harper's Torchbooks; New York: Herder & Herder.

New Directions in Theology Today. William Hordern, gen. ed. Philadelphia: The Westminster Press.

New Frontiers in Theology. Ed. James M. Robinson and John B. Cobb, Jr. New York: Harper & Row, 1963, 1964, 1967.

New Theology. Ed. Martin E. Marty and Dean G. Peerman. New York: The Macmillan Company.

INDEX

Absolute(s), 50, 163
Accrediting, 72, 137-43
Adoptionist, 131
Aeneas, 43
Age of Absolutism, 50
Ambiguity, 18, 20, 74
Analogy, 34, 91, 123, 133, 164
Anarchy, 50
Ancient, 98, 110
Anglicans, 16, 52-53
Anselm, 69
Anti-Christ, 63
Antisemitism, 142
Antiquity, 40, 94, 142
Aquinas, 37, 38, 41, 69
Aristotle, 33, 45, 46, 65, 66
Arminian, 148
Art, 26, 27, 67, 106, 107, 108, 152, 153
Assent, 81
Assumptions, 19, 28-35
Astronaut, 116
Atomism, 144
Atonement, 136, 137
Augustine, 38, 39, 43, 44, 45, 63, 69, 100, 115, 116, 128, 144
Authentic, 24, 91, 97, 165
Authority, 35, 58, 74, 98

Baptist, 77
Barth, Karl, 24, 55, 105, 154

Becker, Carl, 41, 45
Being, plentitude of, 23, 27
Believe in order to understand, 69
Believers, 93, 150
Biblical, 87, 160
Bishops, 75, 76
Blood of the martyrs, 114
Book of Concord, 82
Book of knowledge, 74, 98, 99
Book of Nature, 51
Book of Scripture, 51
Boundaries, 121-24
Brinton, Crane, 41

Cage, John, 154
Calvin, 38, 39, 41, 45, 48, 52, 55, 64, 65, 70, 73, 74, 78, 91, 97, 99, 100, 102, 109, 137, 142, 144-48
Cataclysmic, 30
Catechisms, 82
Cathedral(s), 101, 164
Charisma, 75, 76, 77, 149
Children, 164
Christological, 106, 119, 122, 125, 129-34
Church, 46, 57, 92, 94, 95, 103, 134, 151, 162-64
Church buildings, 164
Church historians, 15
Church order, 75-78
Church union, 59, 77

CONTOURS
OF
FAITH
Changing Forms
of Christian Thought

JOHN
DILLENBERGER

If today's theology is to be faithful to its task and meaningful to the majority of human beings, it cannot simply be practiced as in the past. Traditional forms and modes of expression may have to be abandoned because they have lost their original meaning. Intentions behind old forms must be recaptured and their contributions appropriated in means more congenial to modern discourse.

In this work Dr. Dillenberger presents conclusions based upon his research in historical theology and intellectual history. He writes clearly and draws upon a wide range of knowledge and personal insights as he develops his thesis that systematic theology is no longer viable. His case for a historical approach emphasizes that theology in the future may not look anything like the theology we have known. Although the risks are great and the uncertainties perplexing, John Dillenberger's approach is definitely a valid option if theology is to be a part of tomorrow.